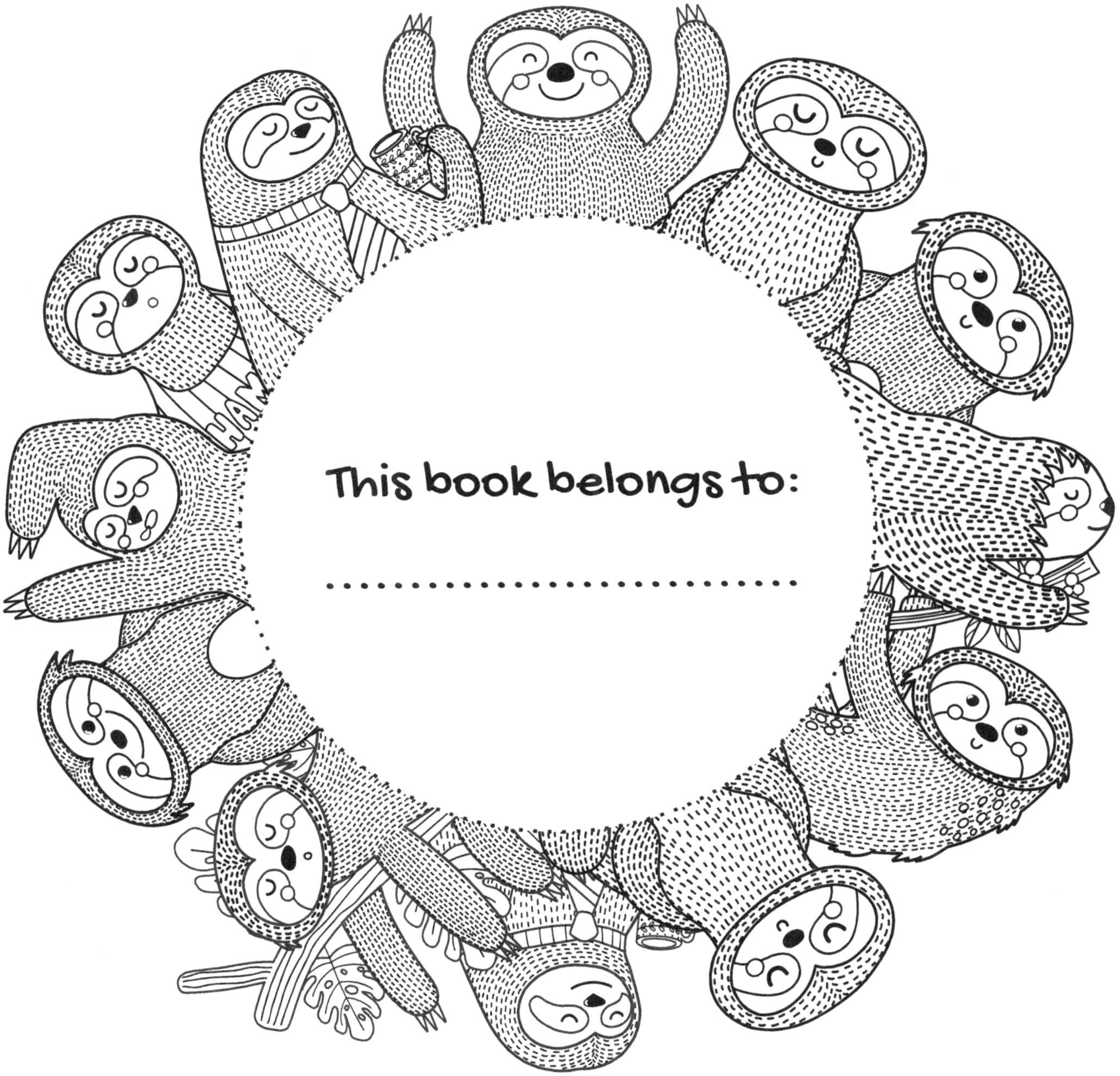

This book belongs to:

....

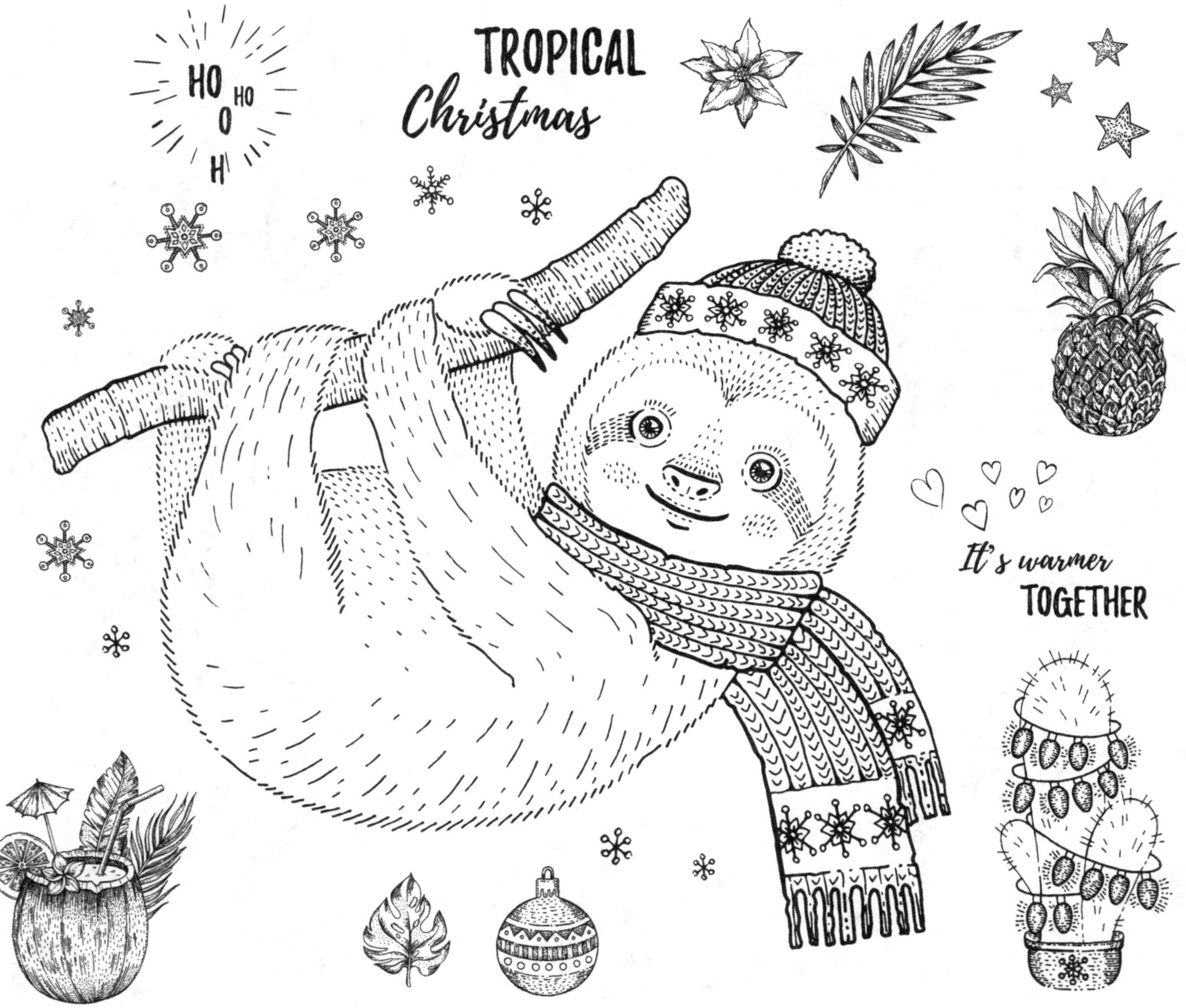

HO HO HO
TROPICAL
Christmas
It's warmer
TOGETHER

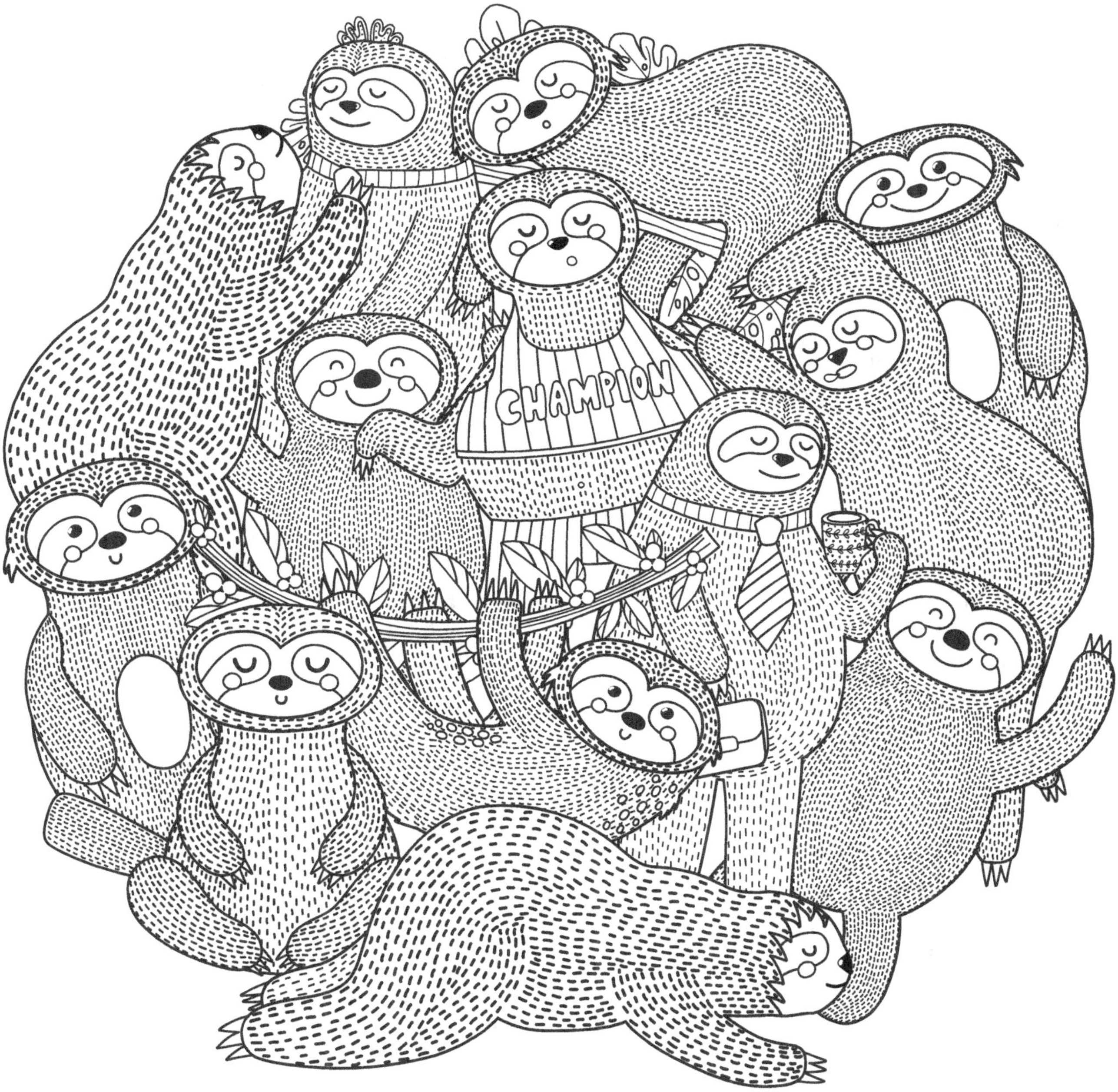
CHAMPION

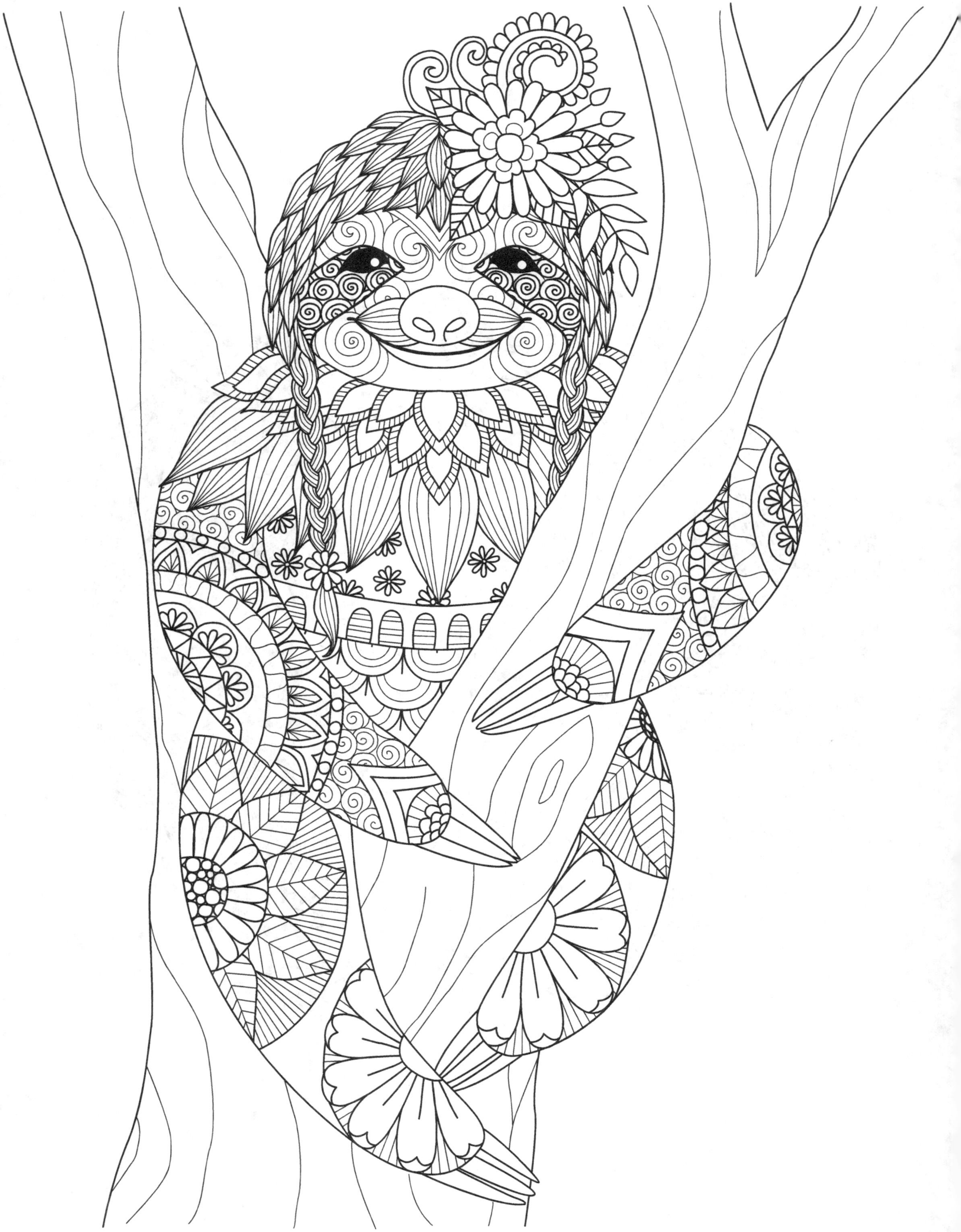

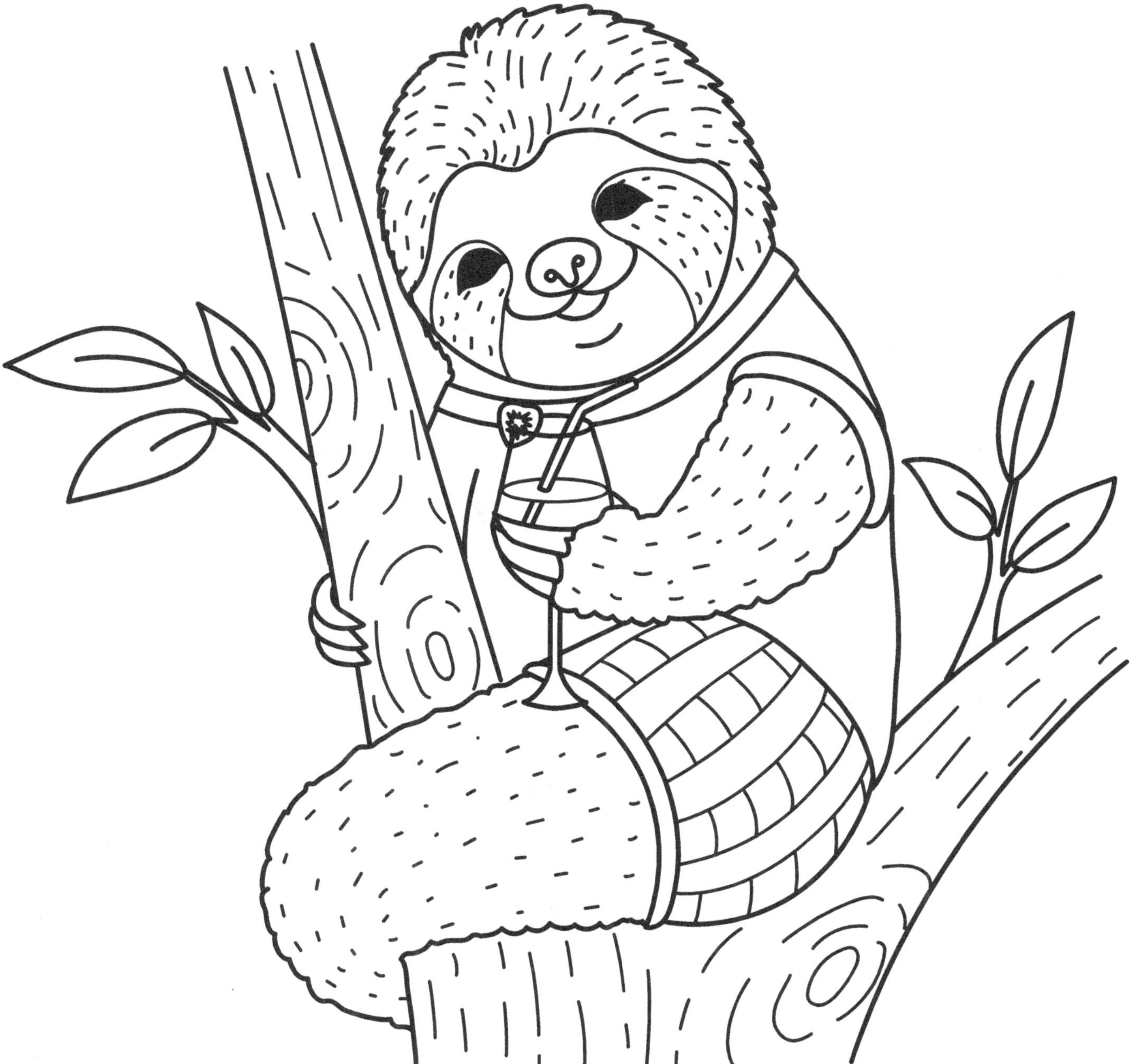

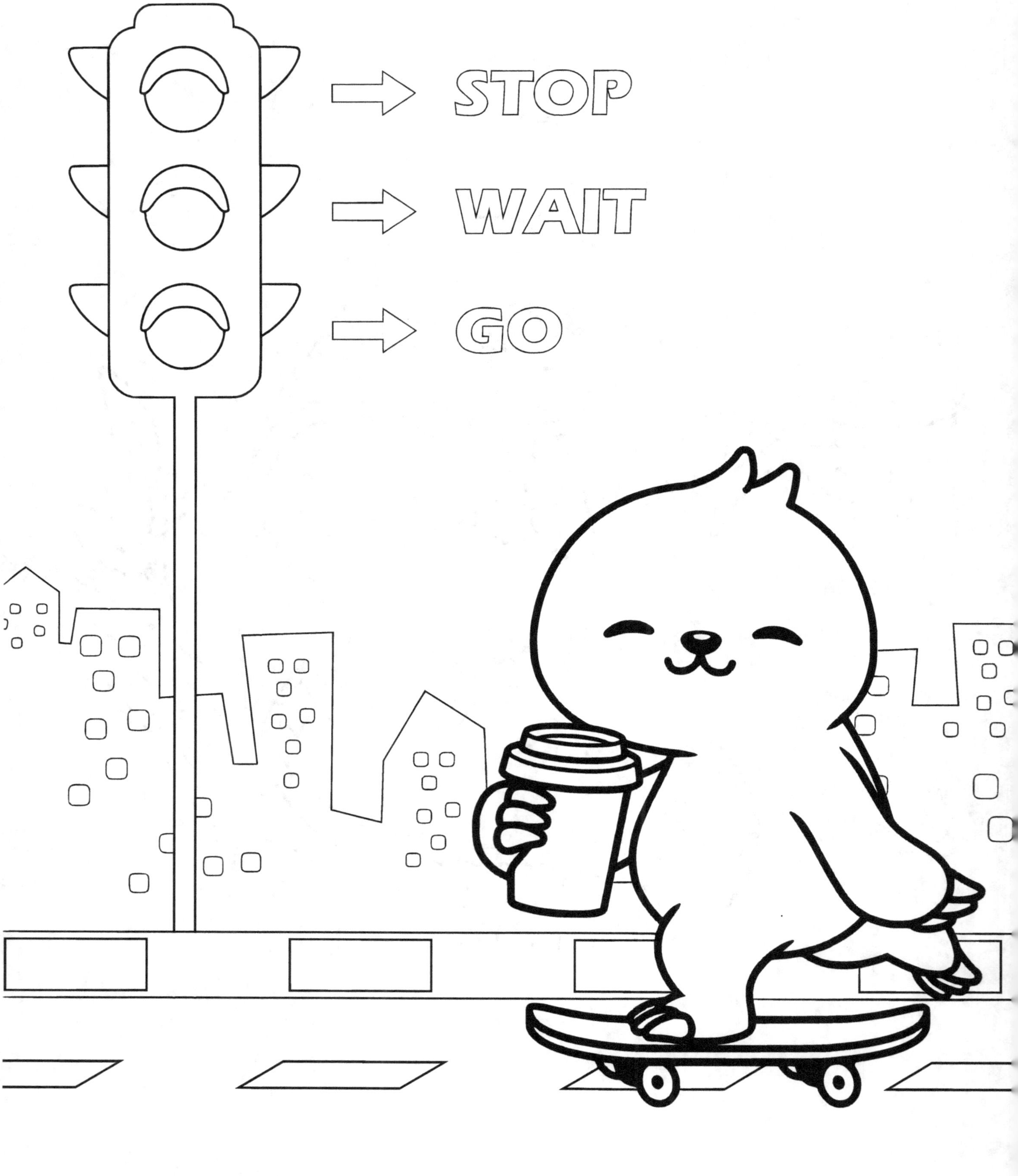
STOP
WAIT
GO

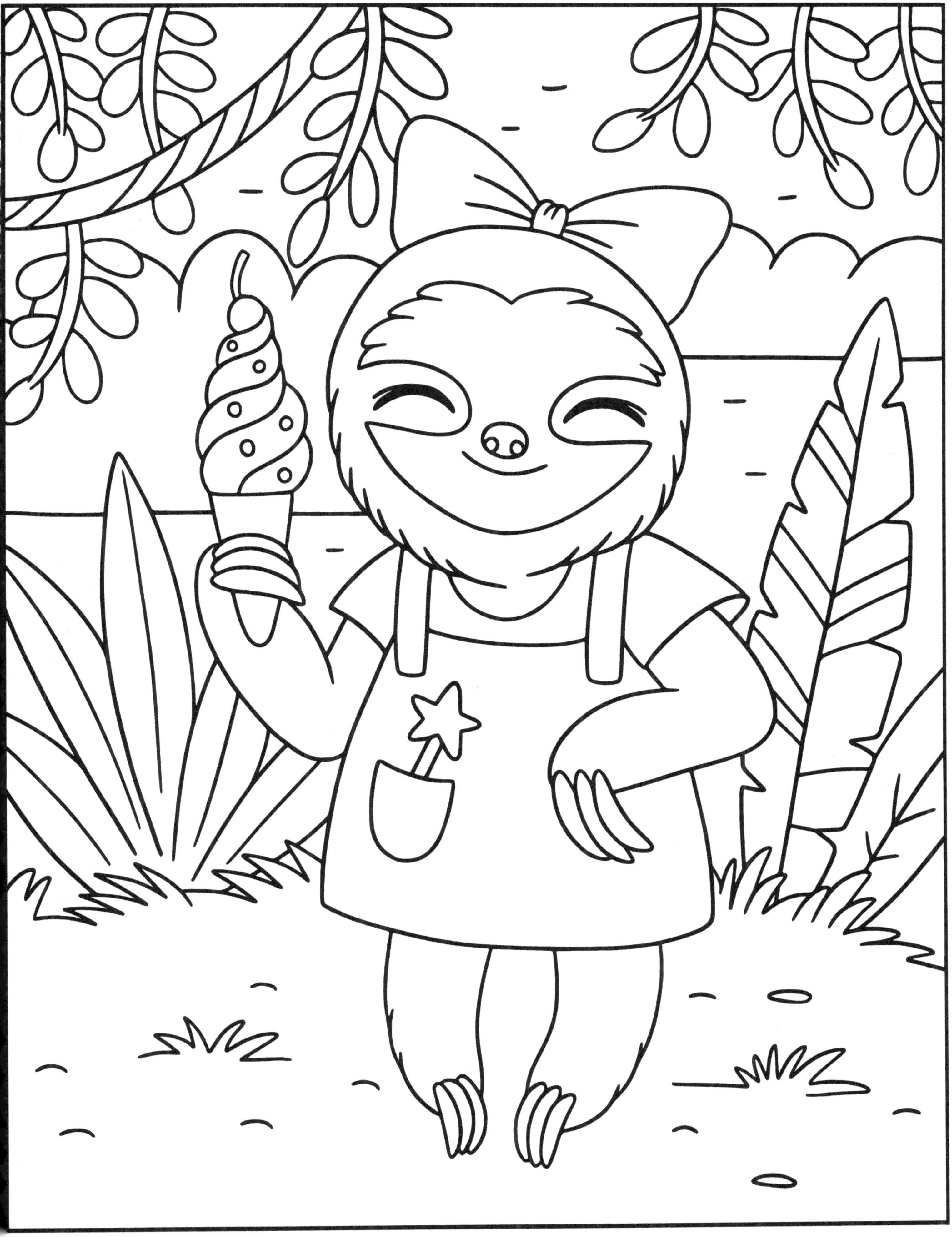

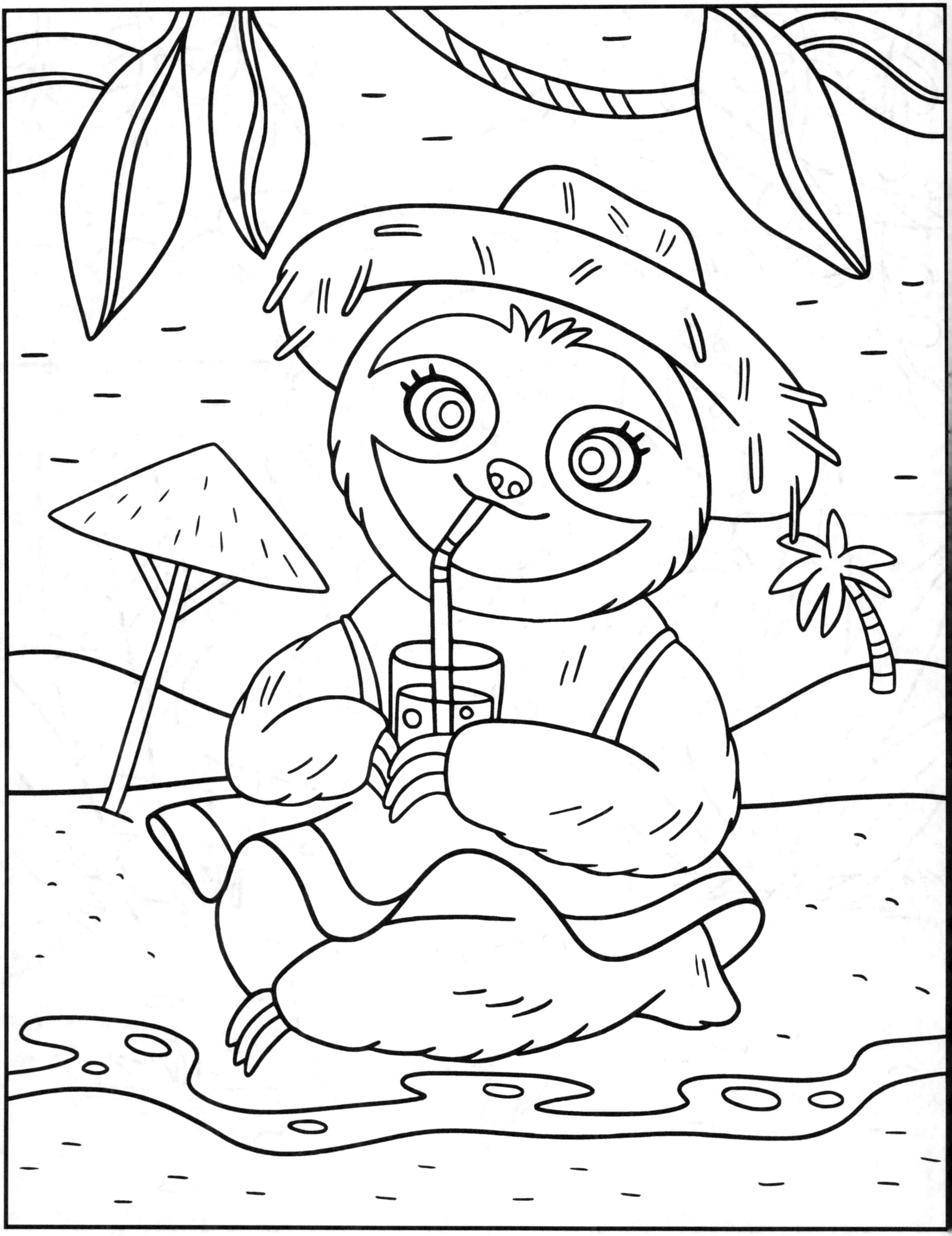

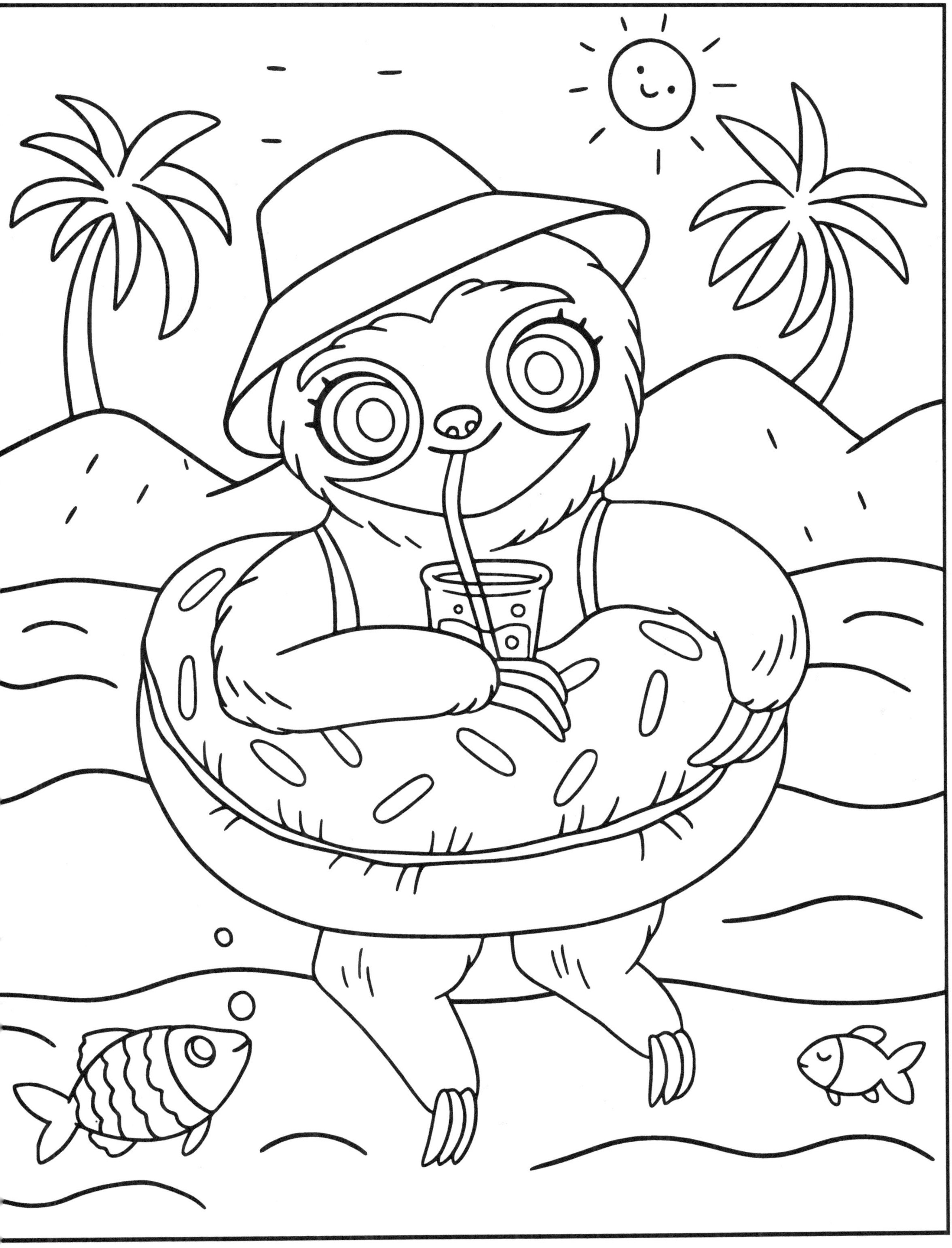

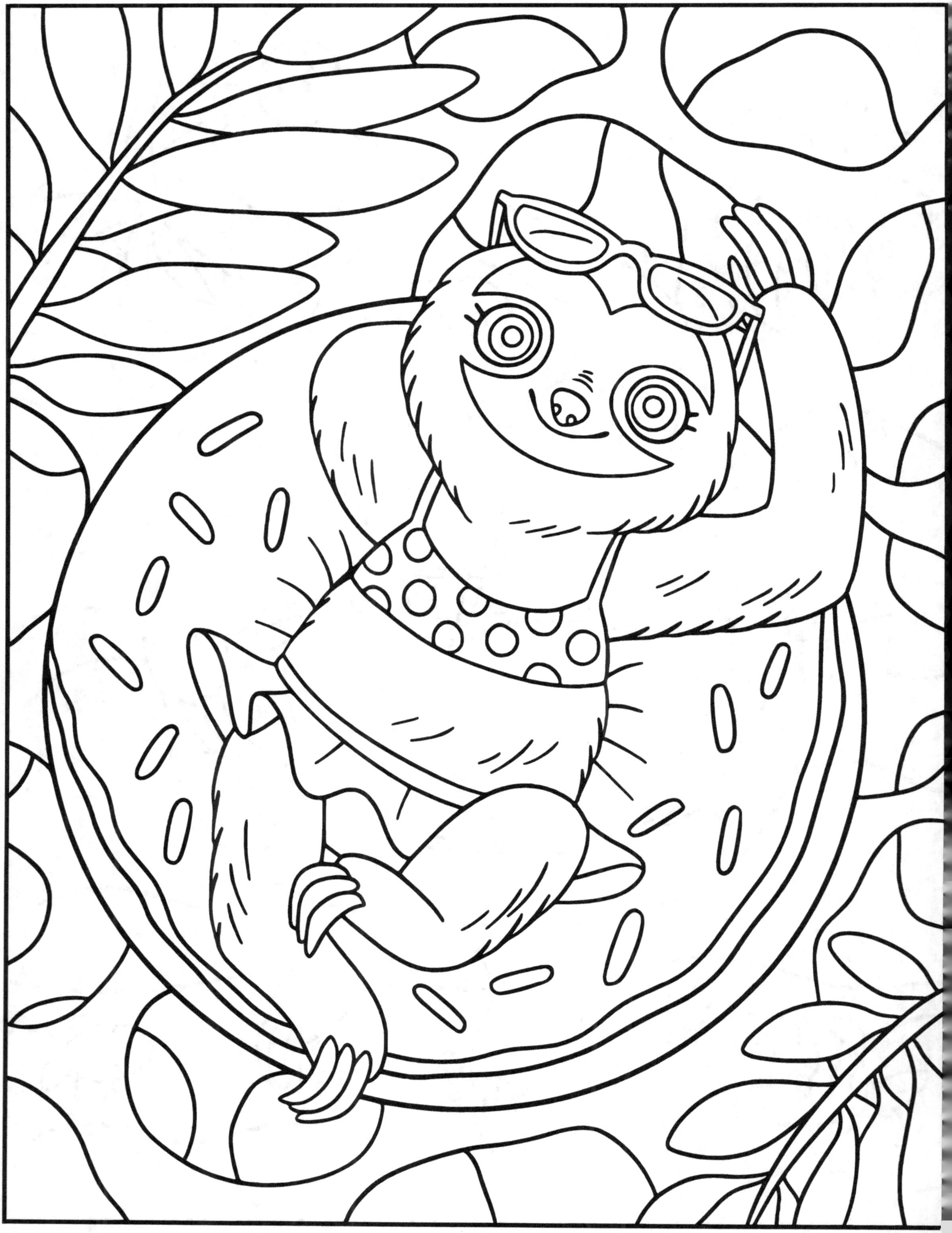

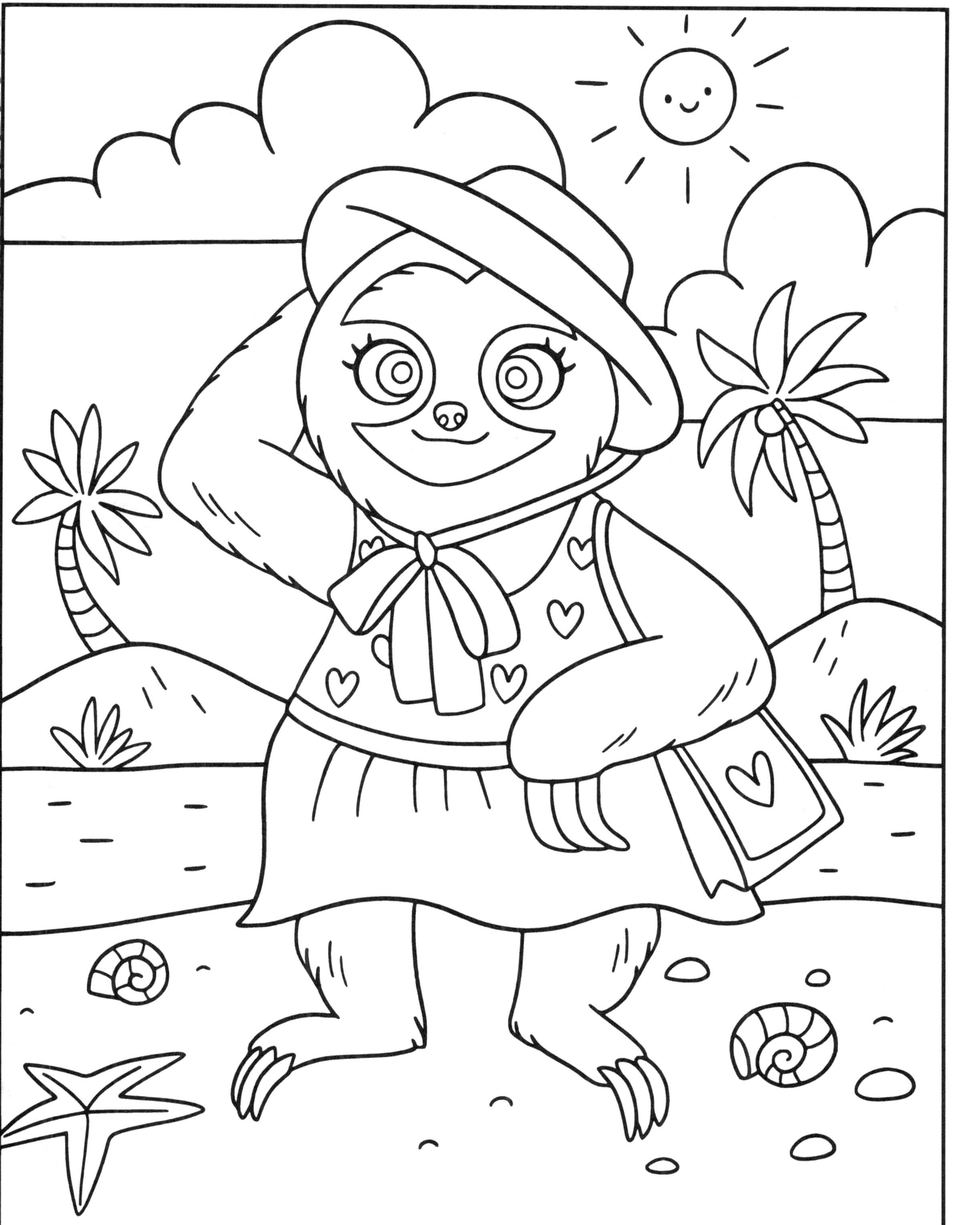

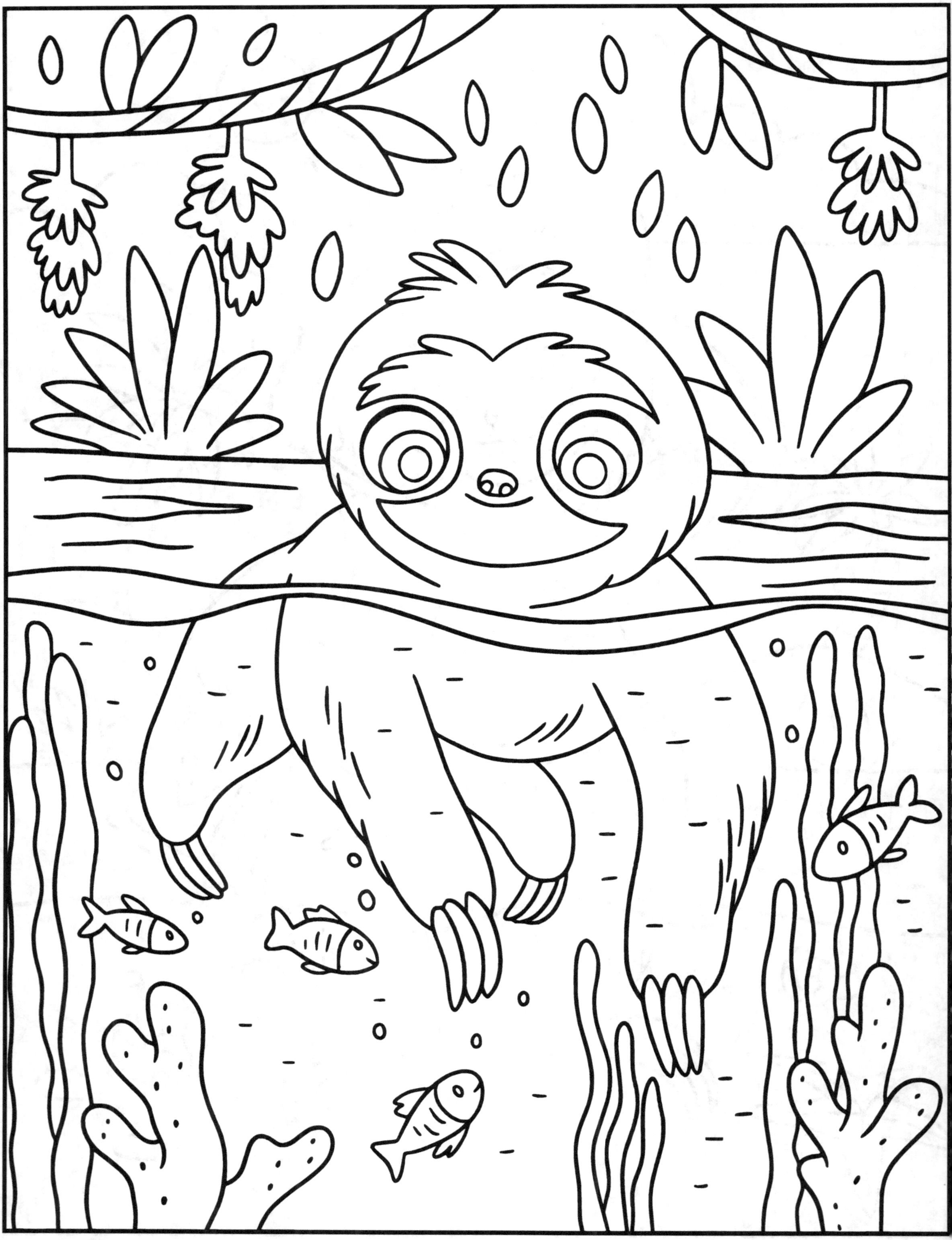

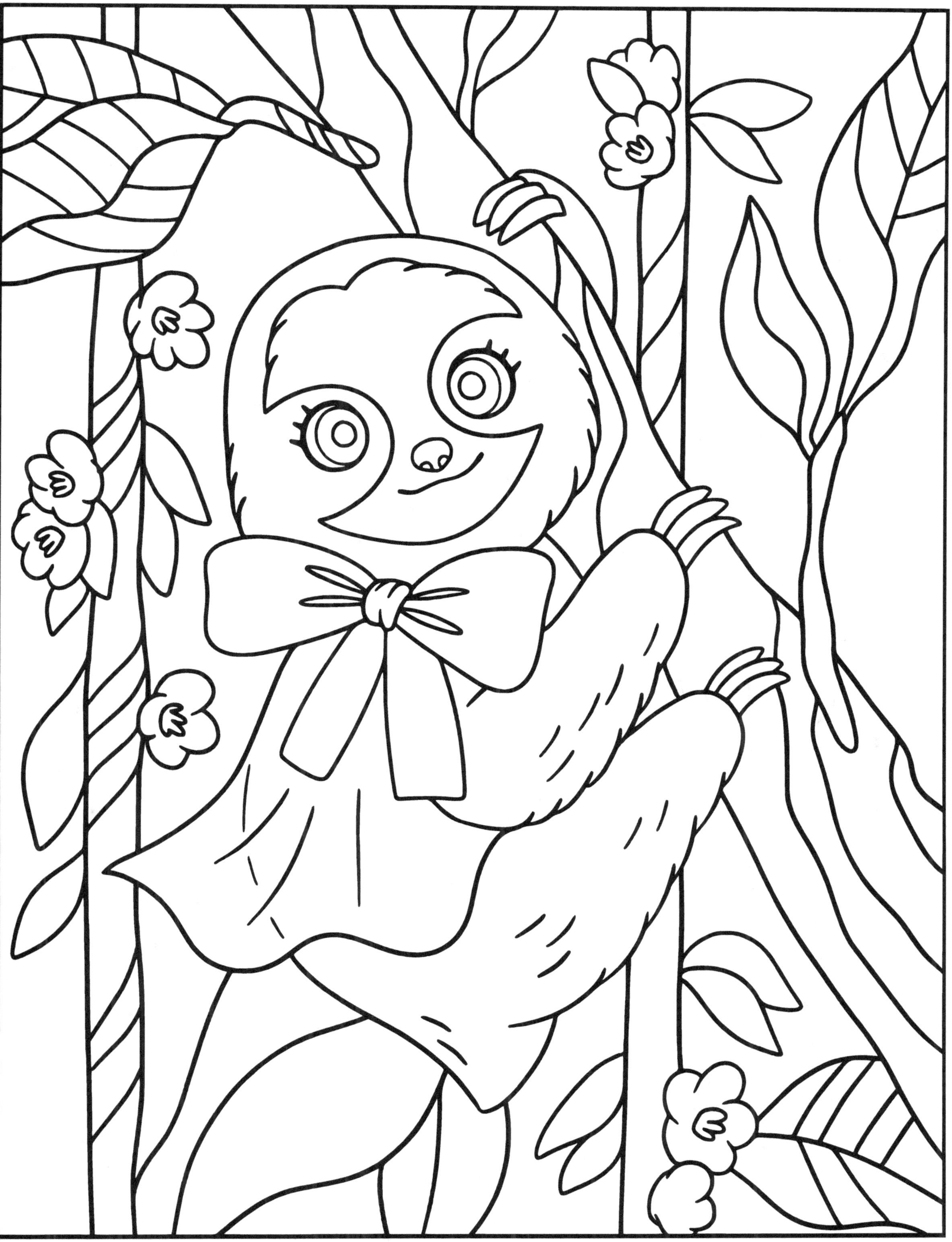

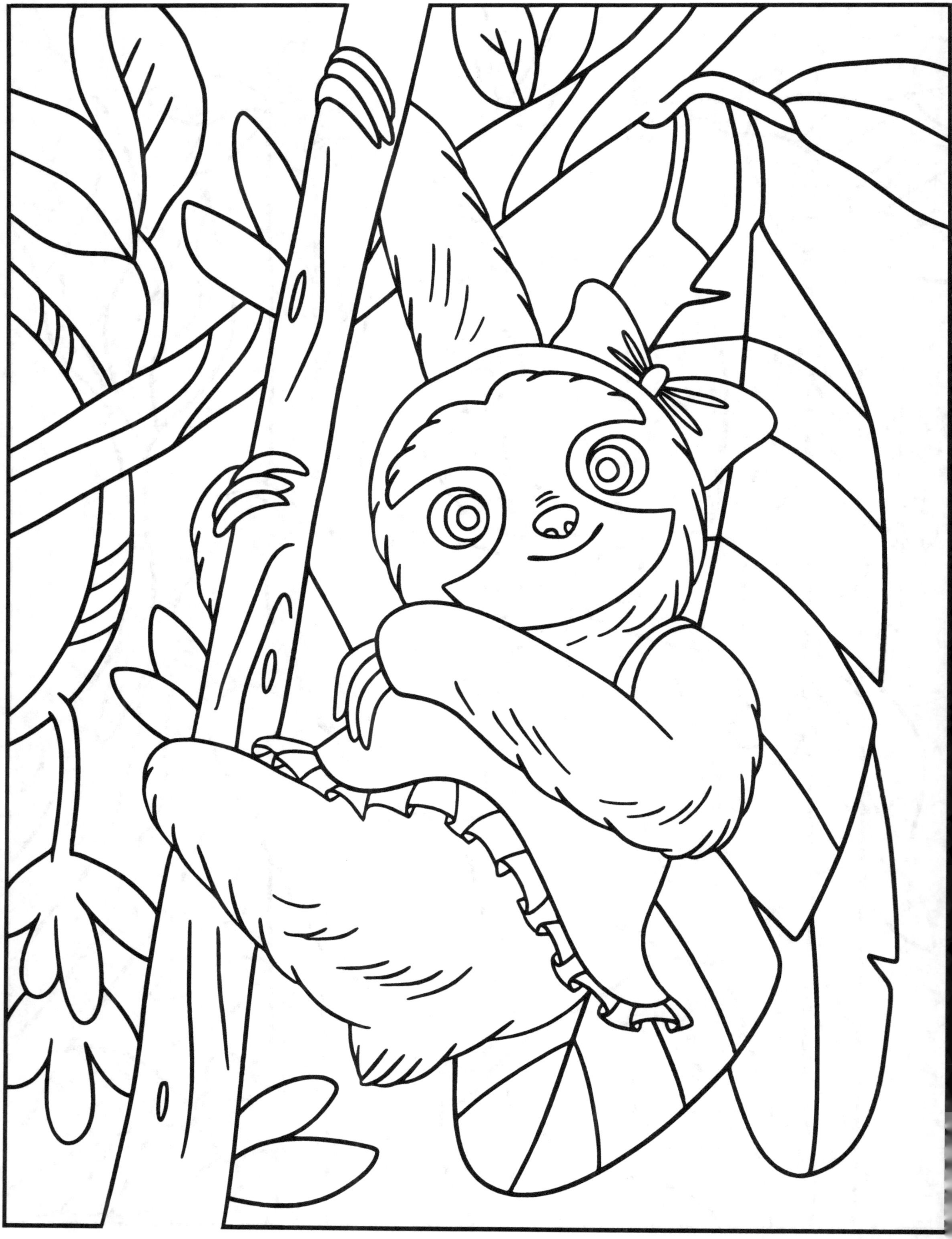

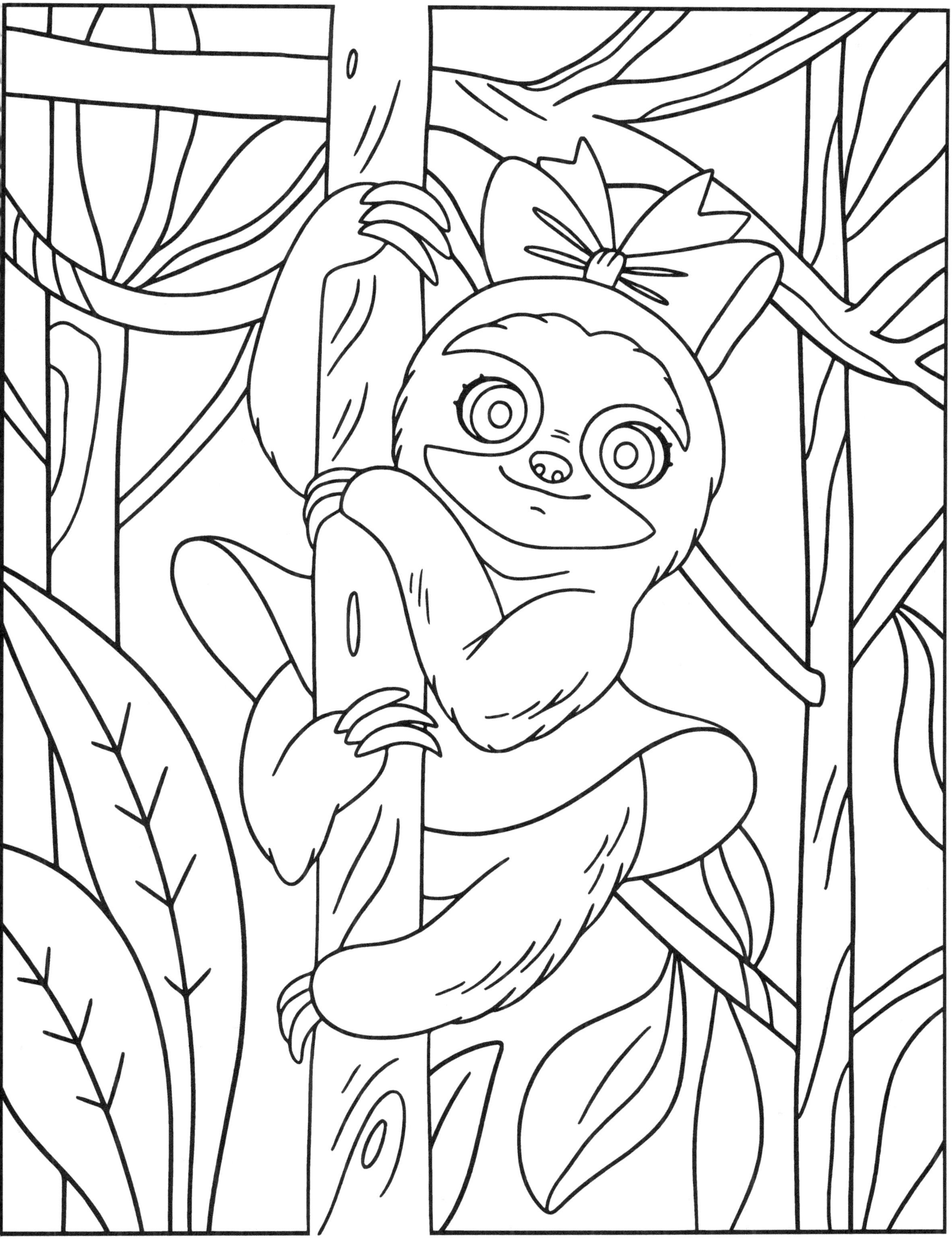

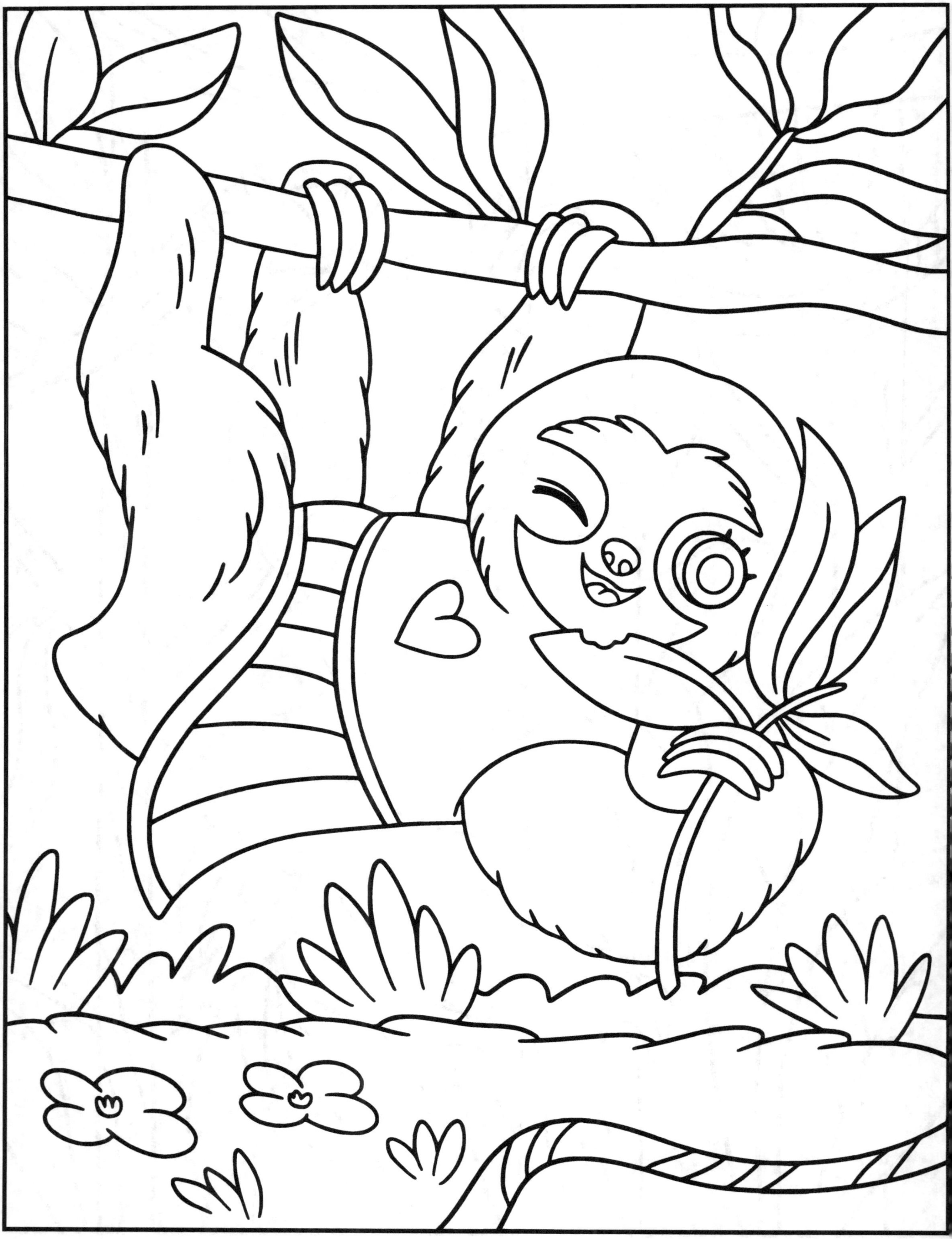

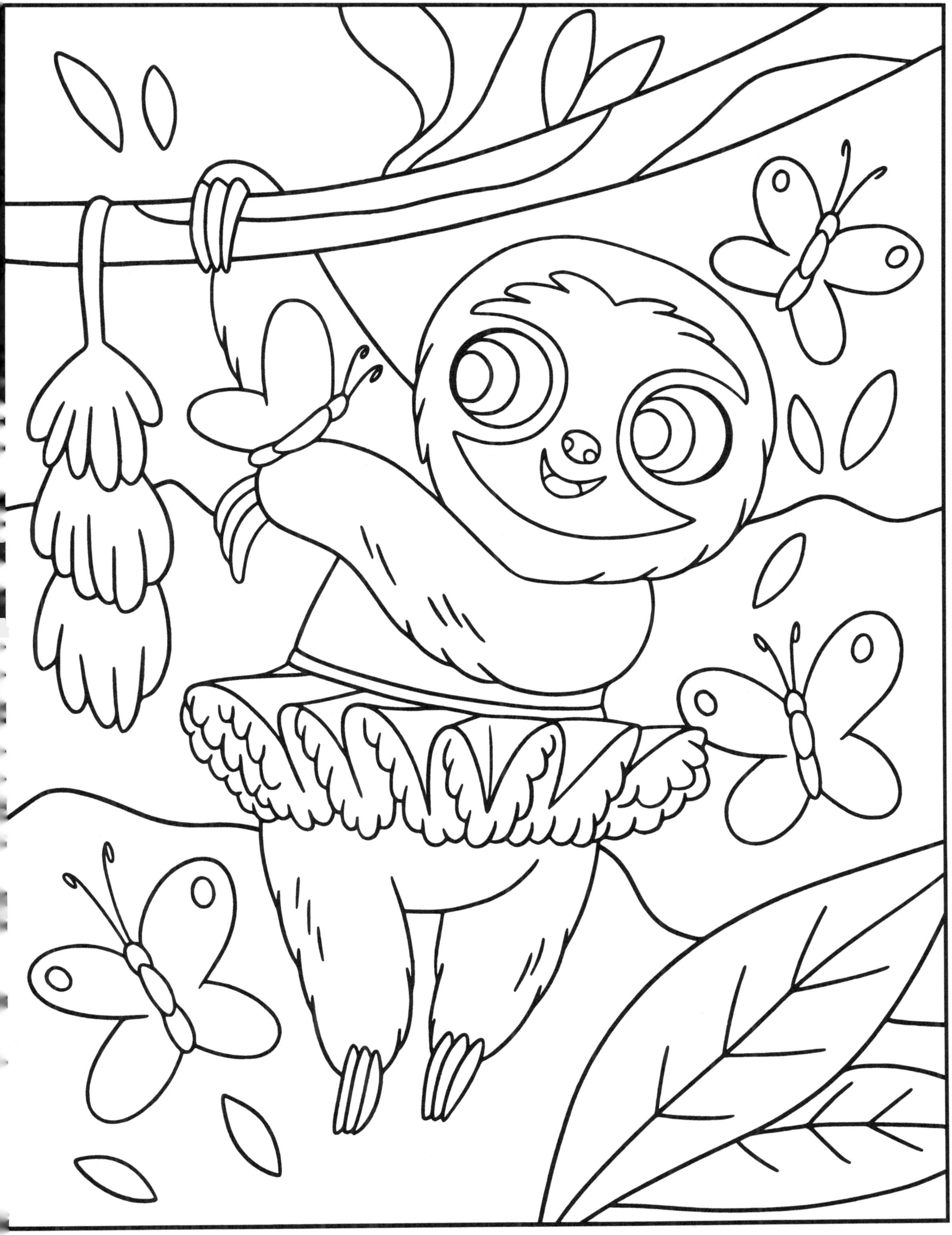

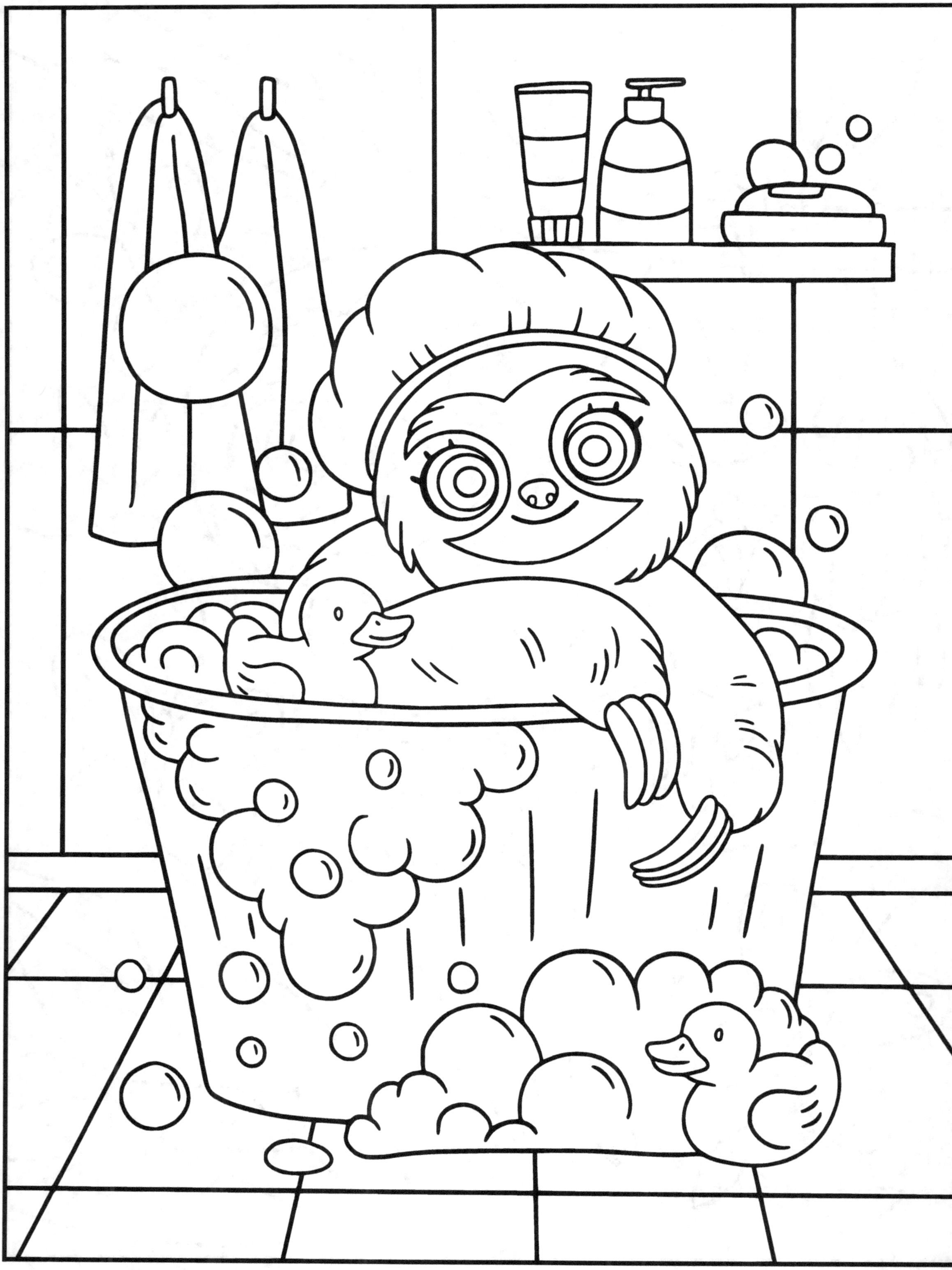

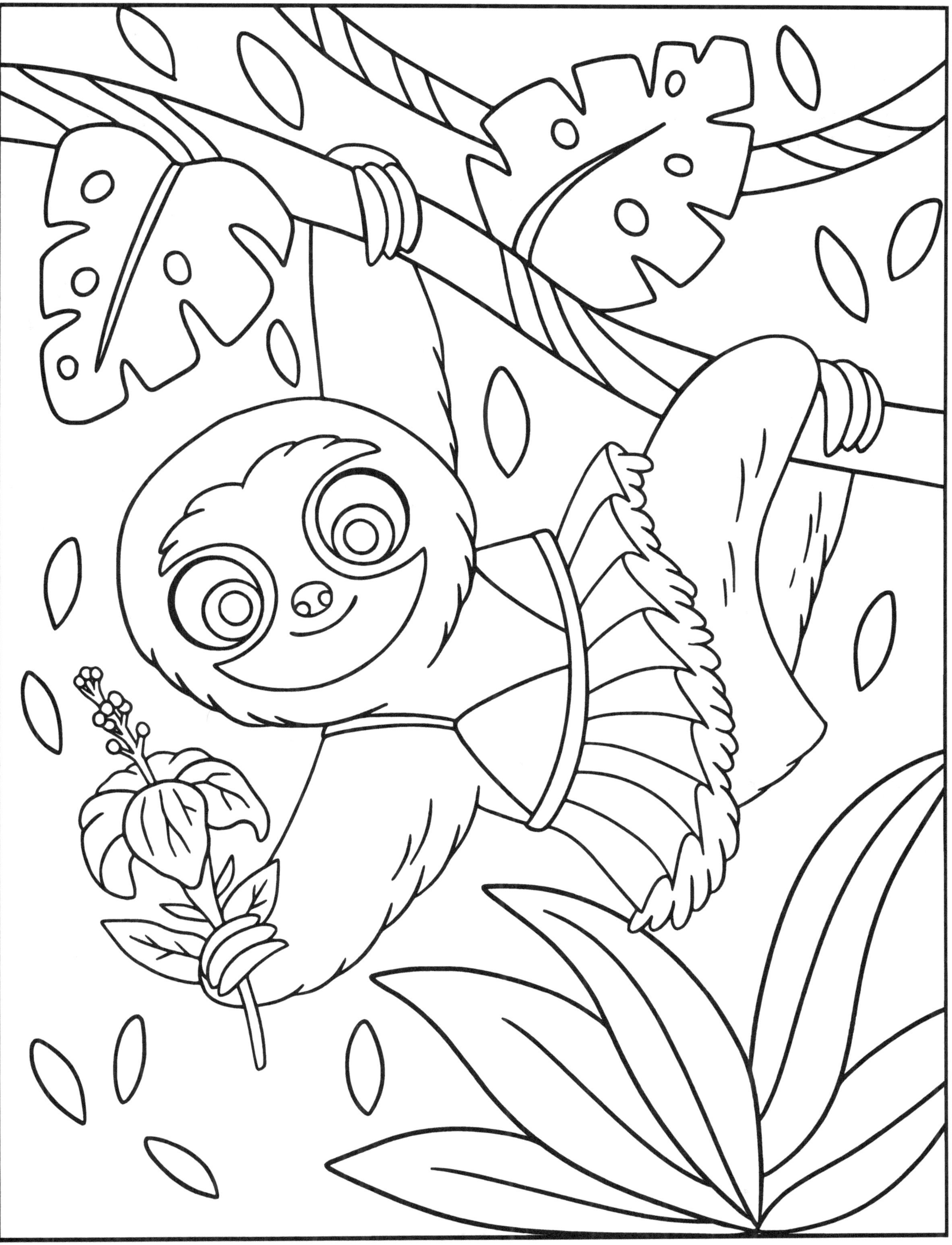

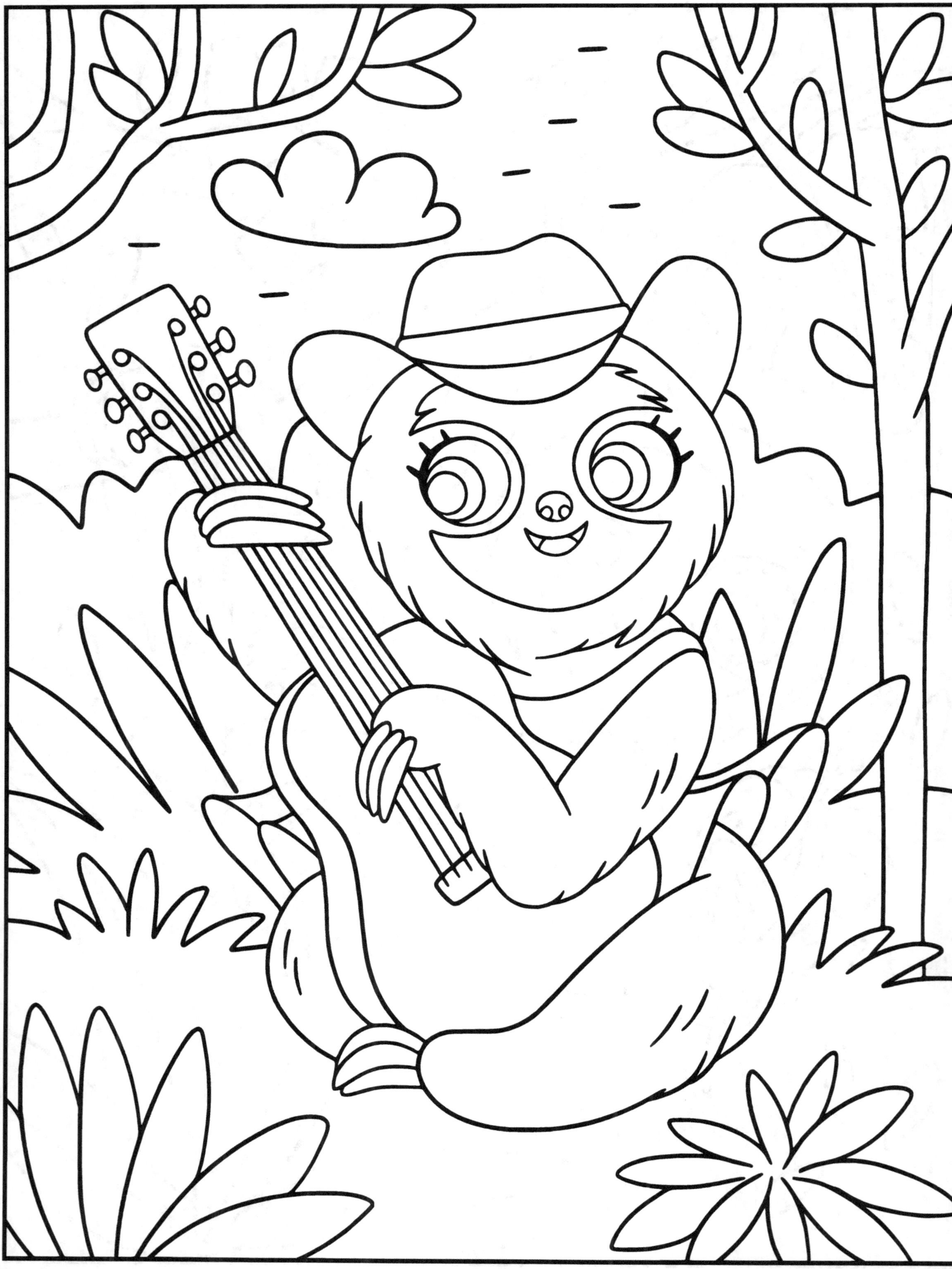

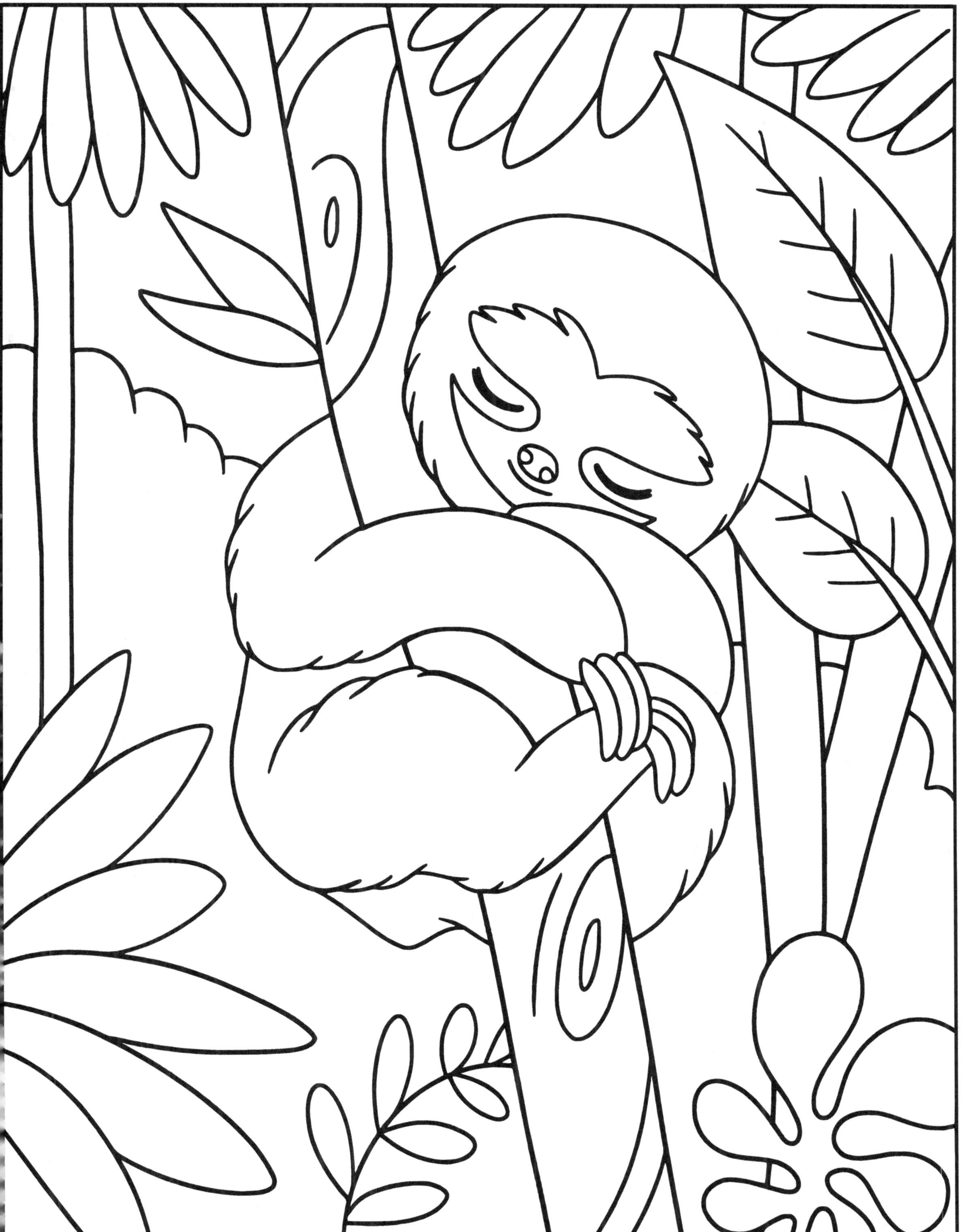

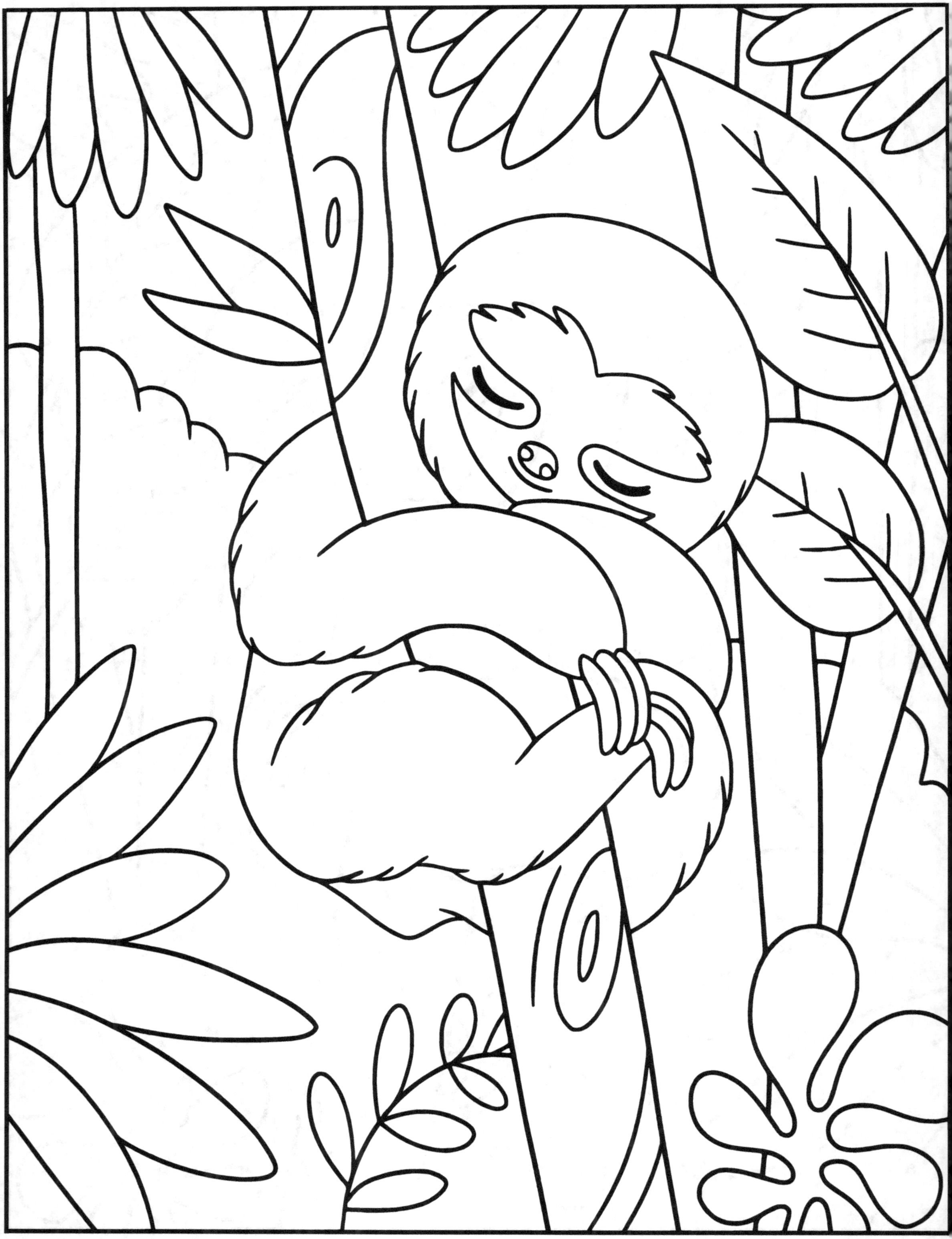

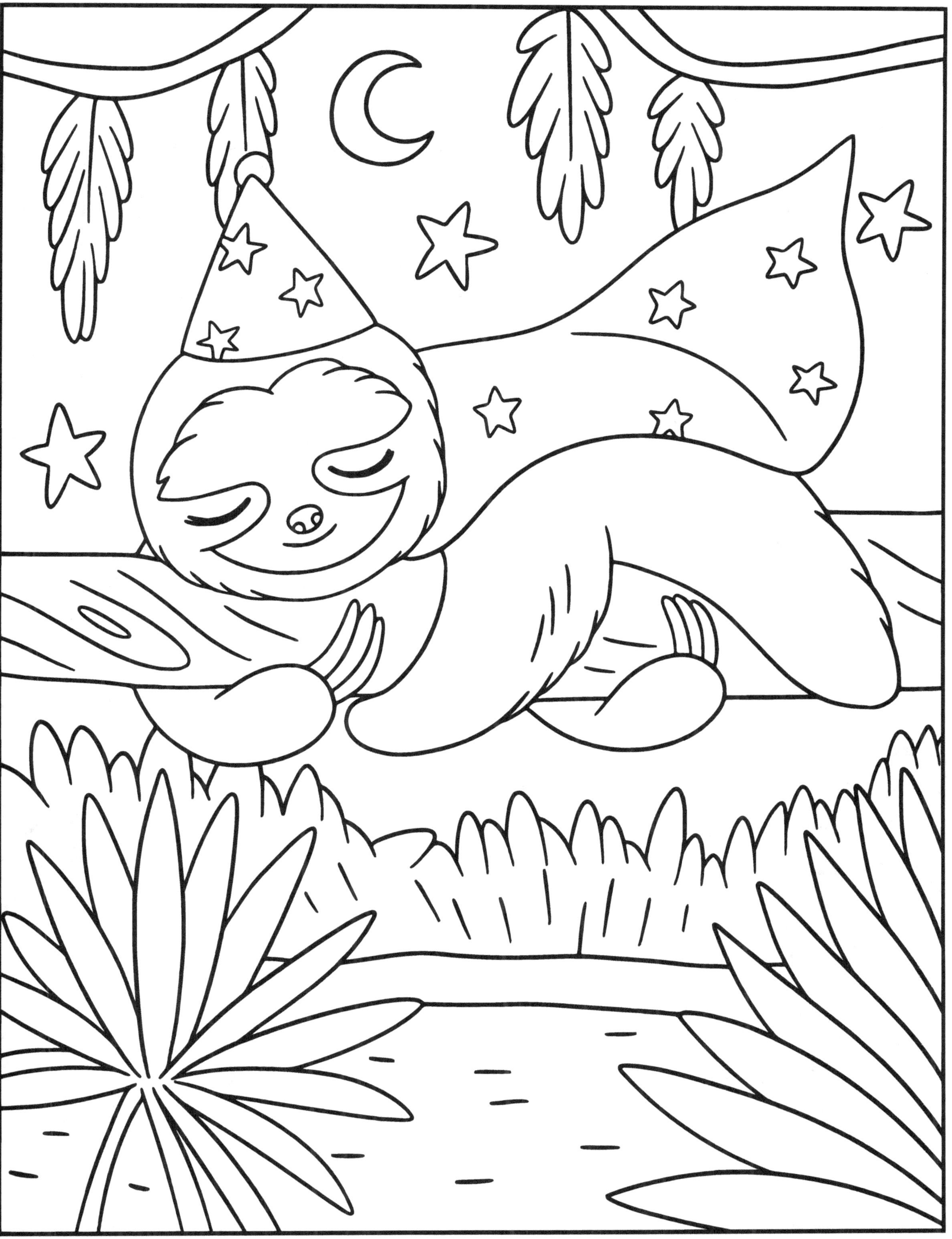

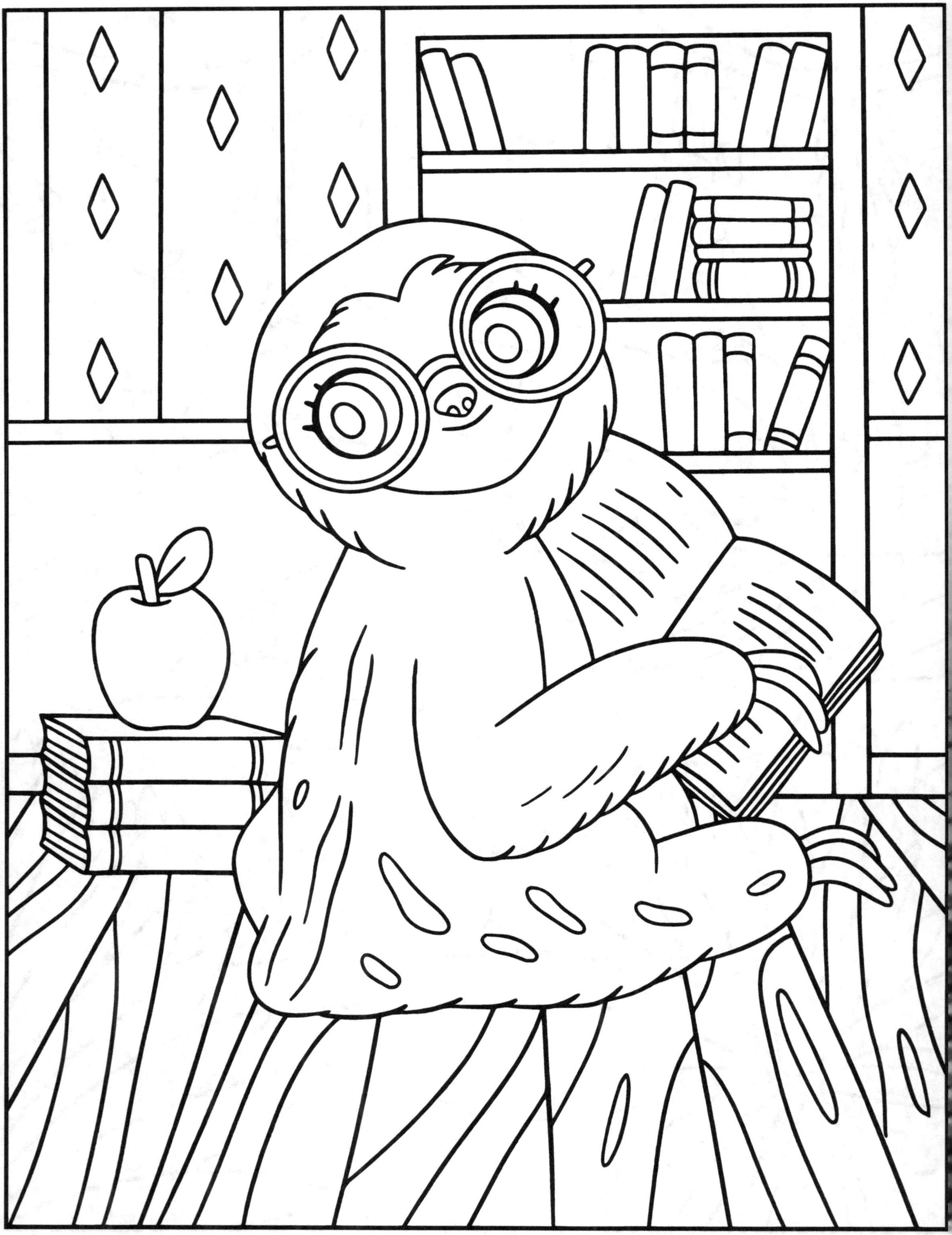

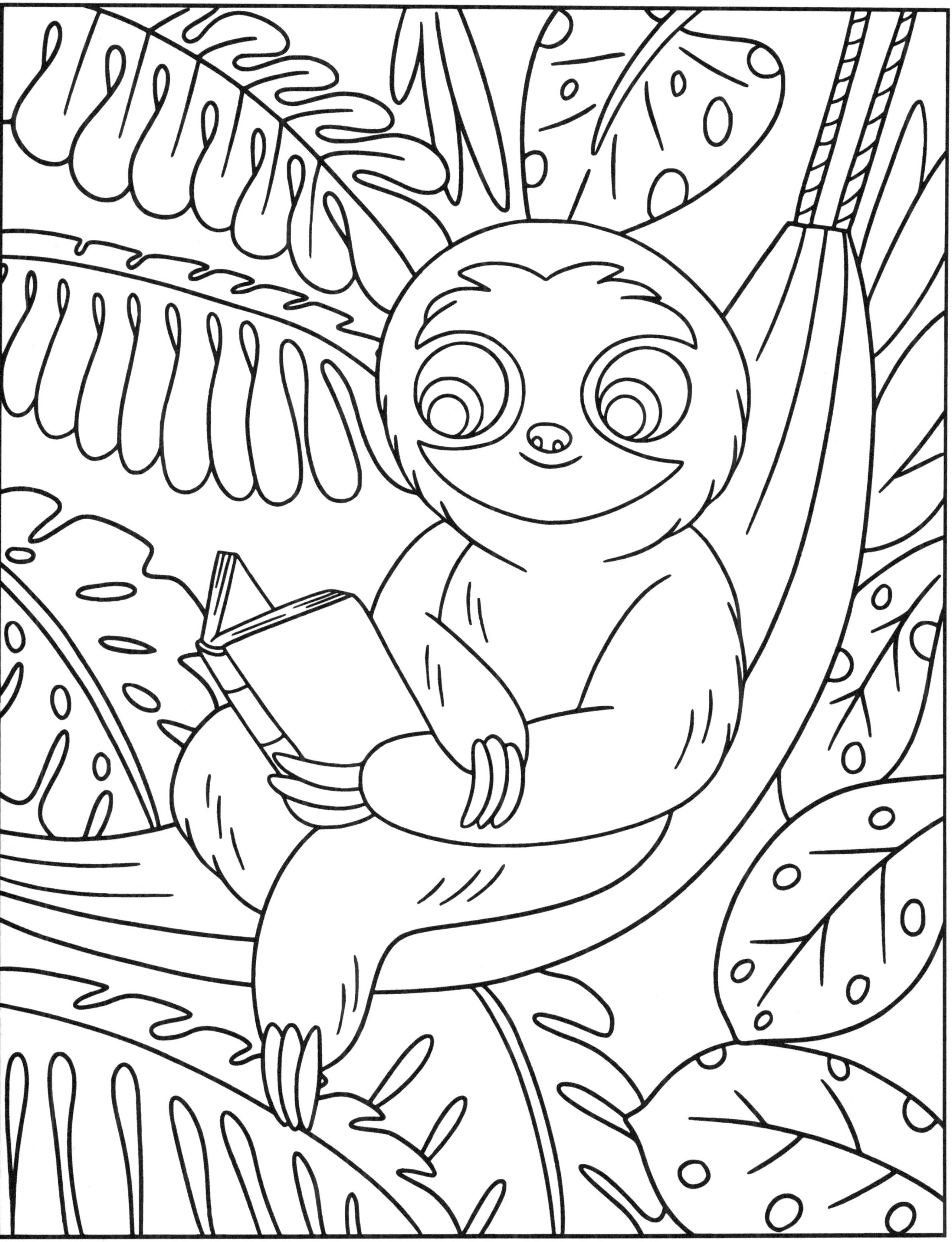

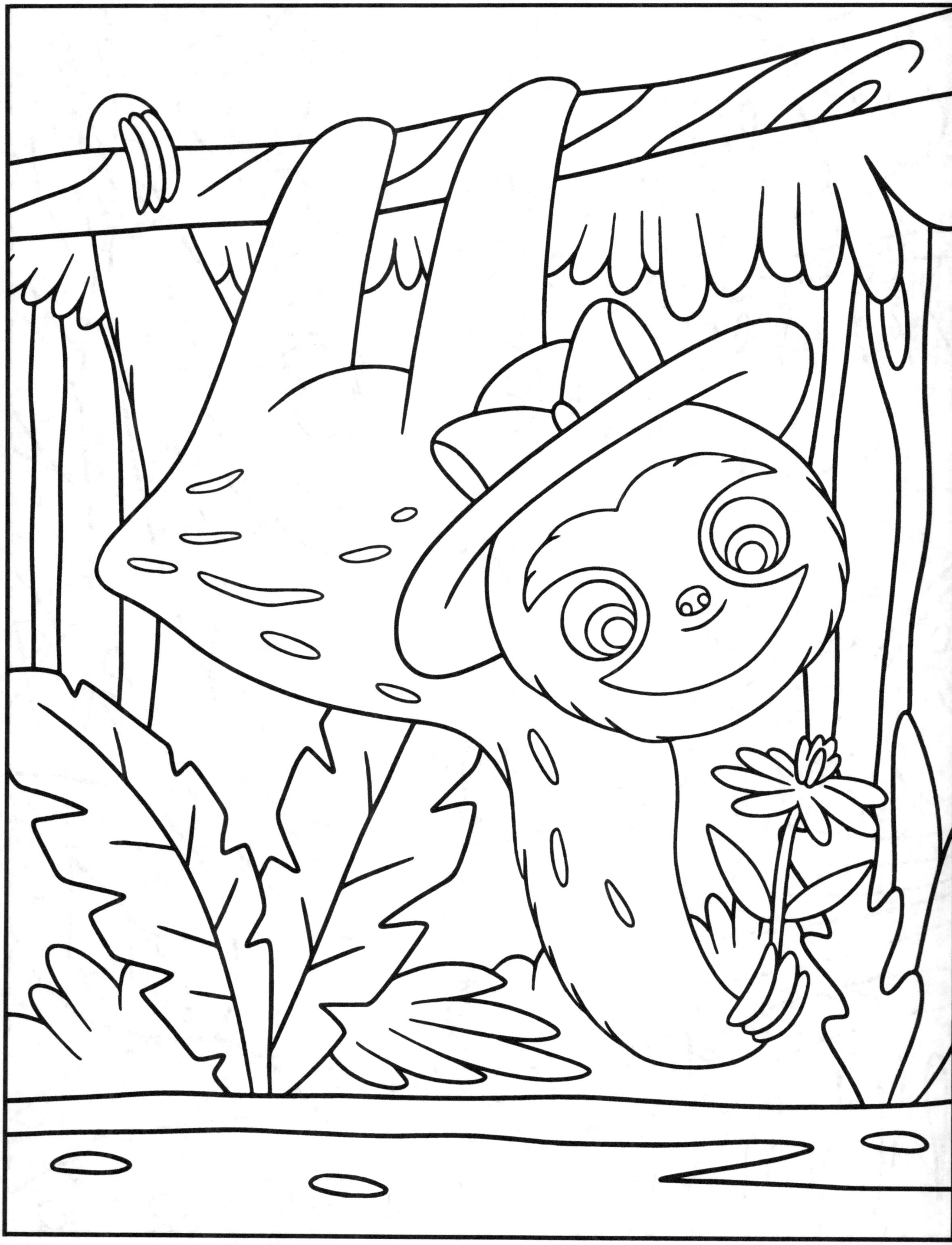

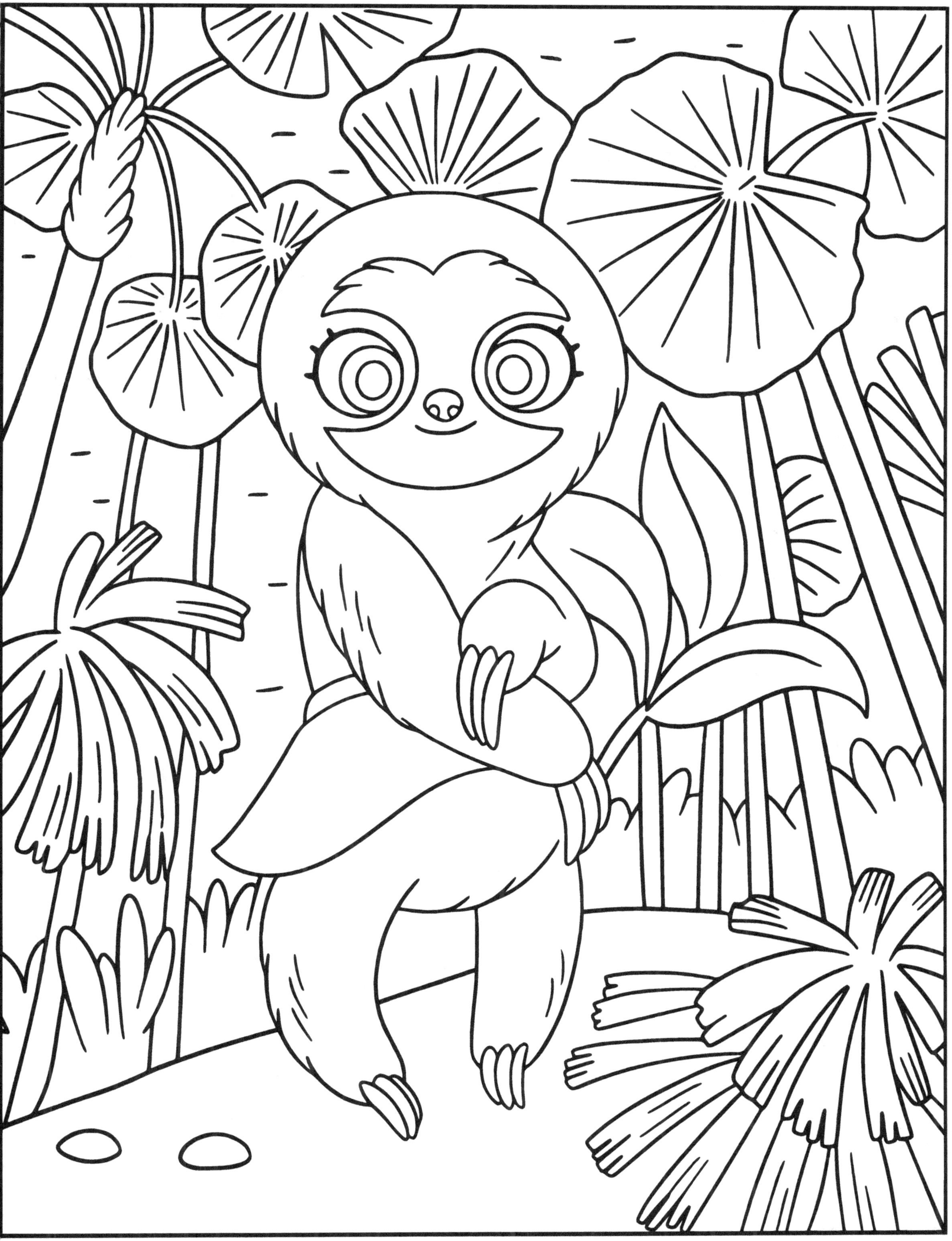

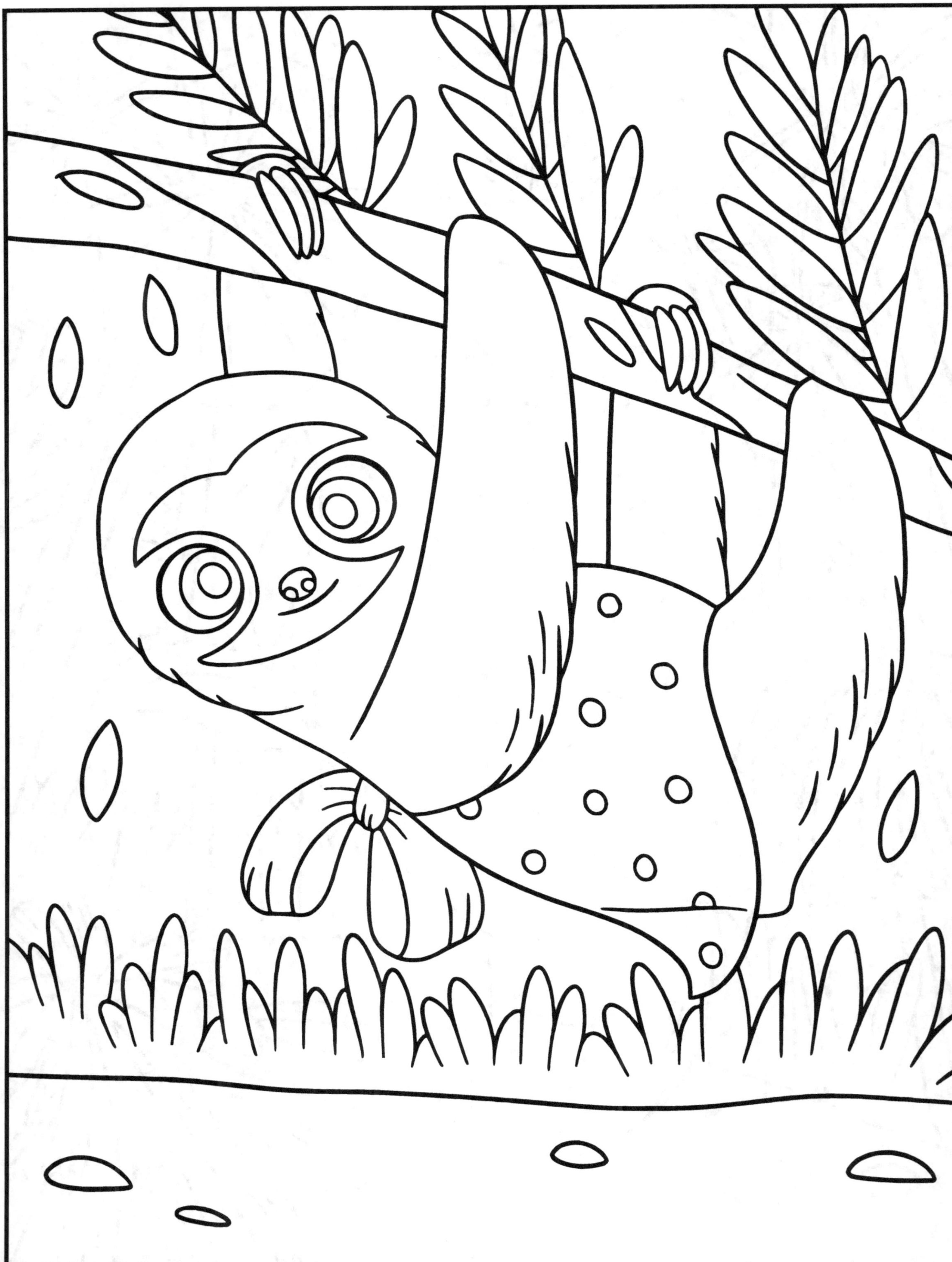

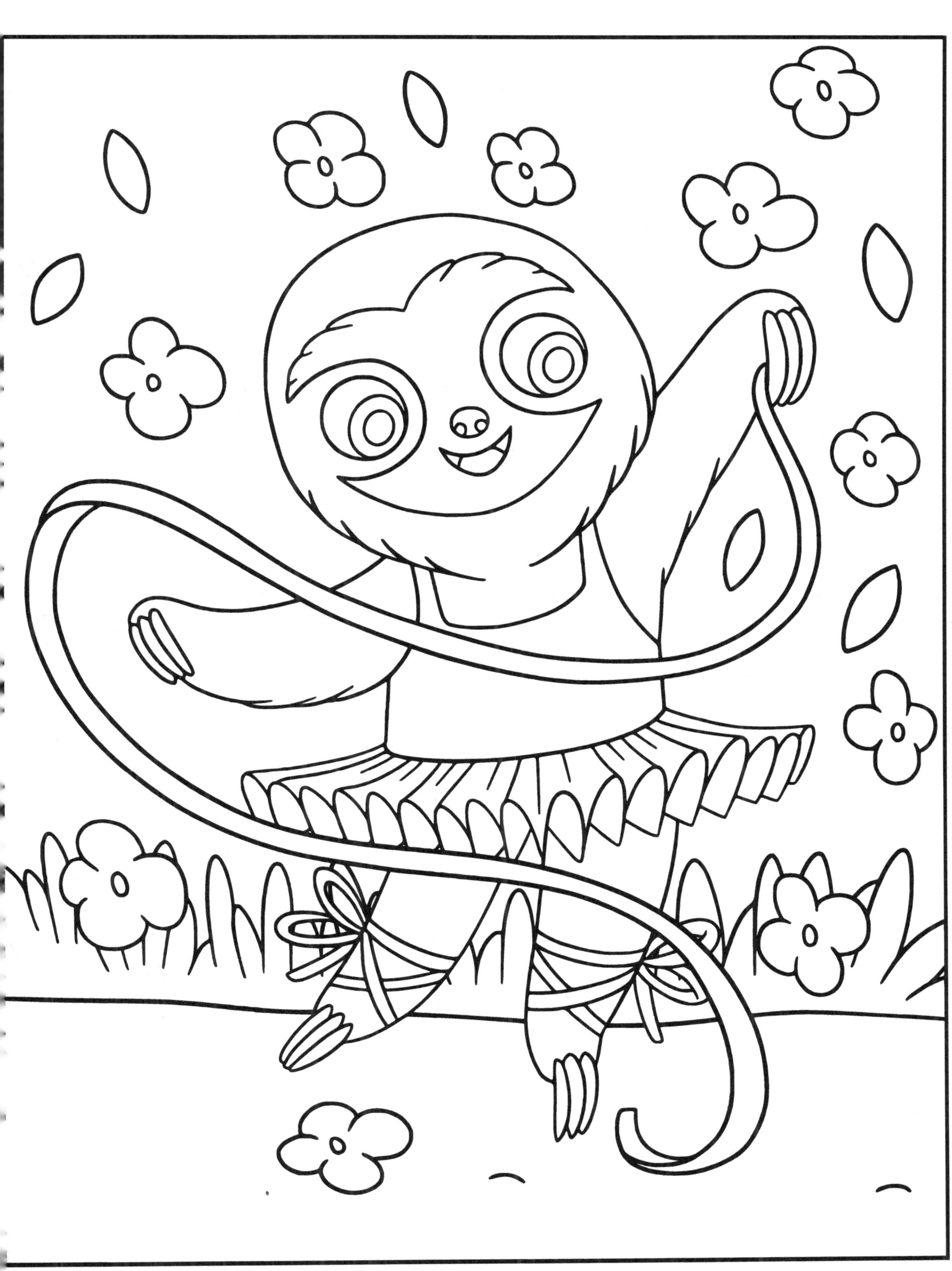

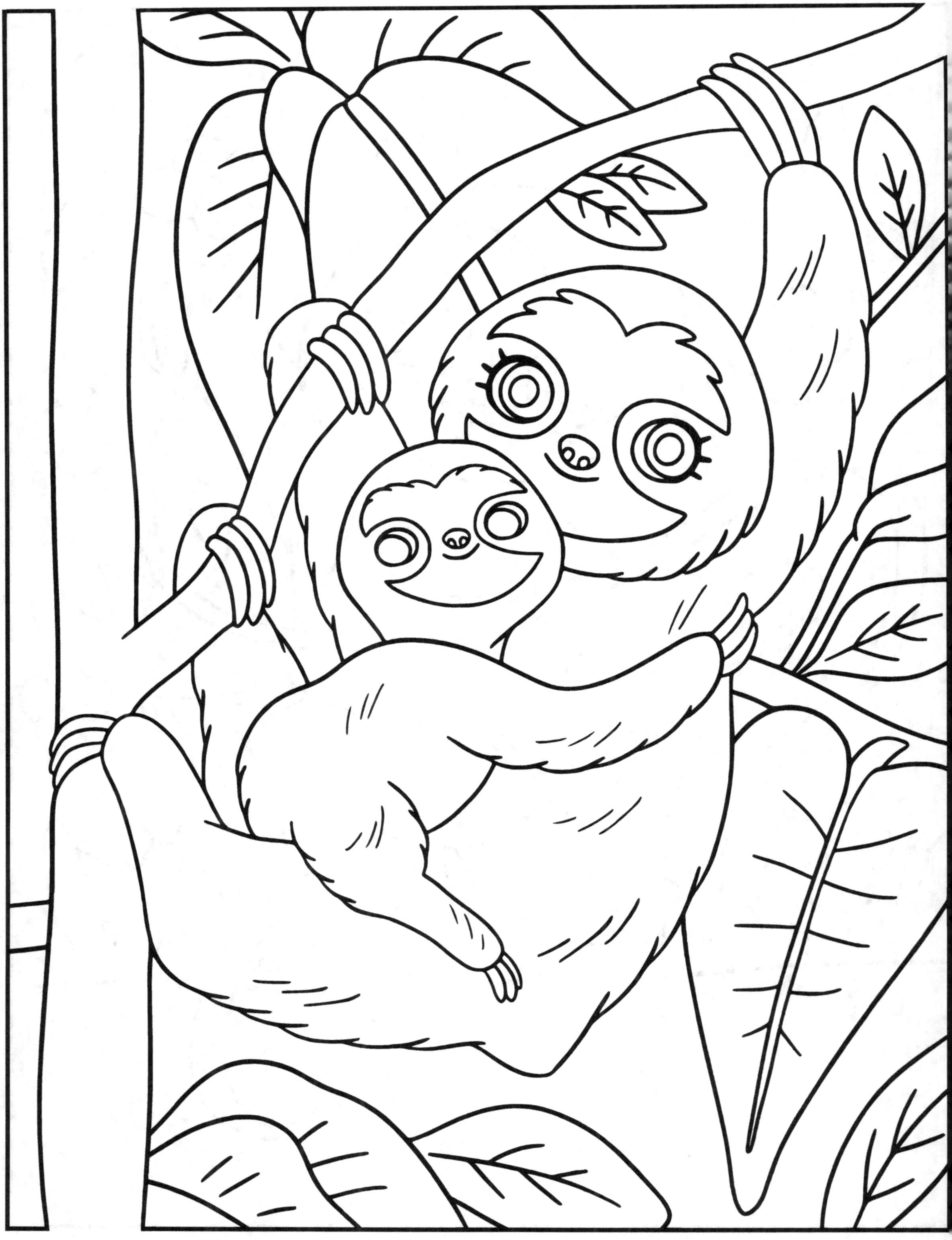

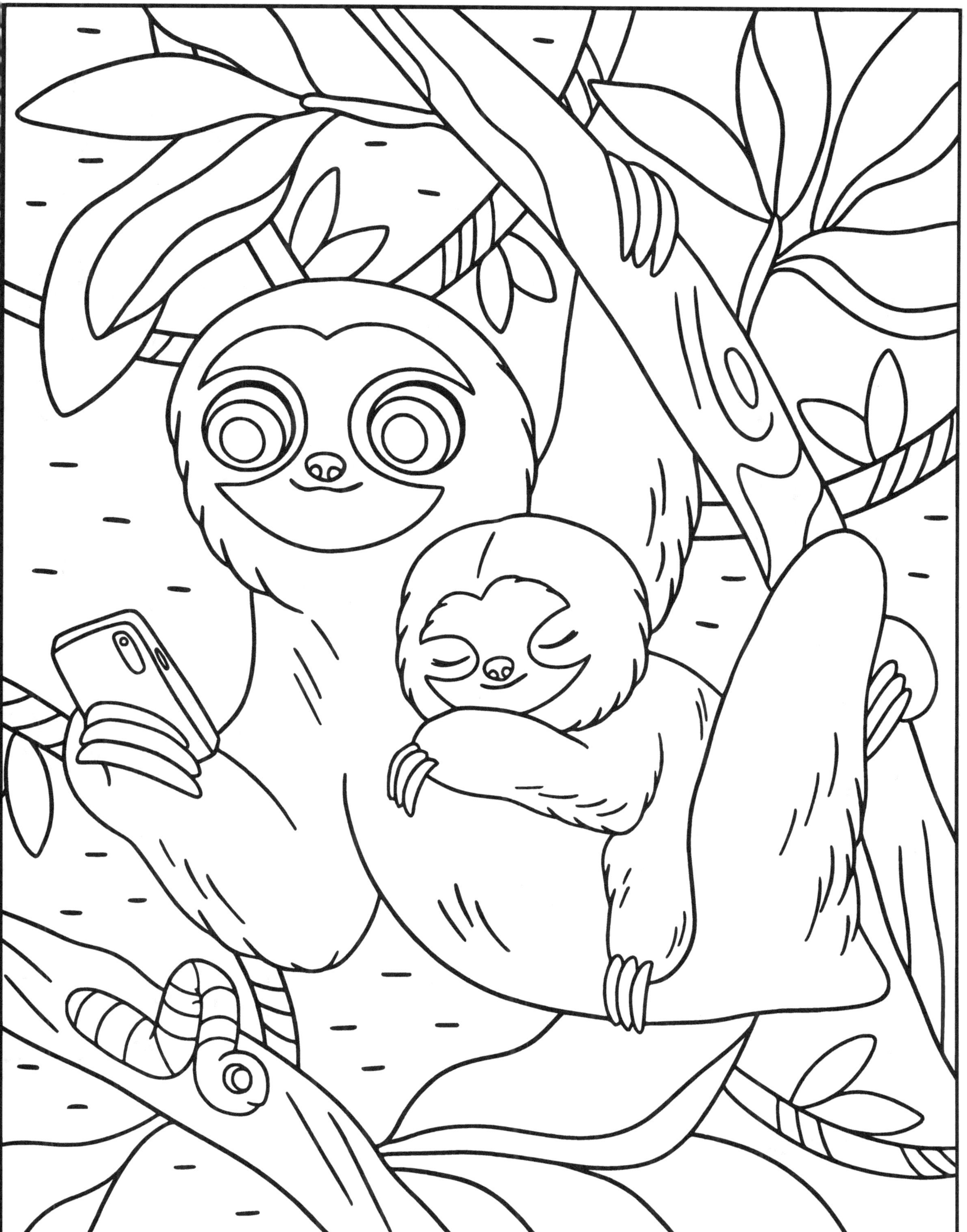

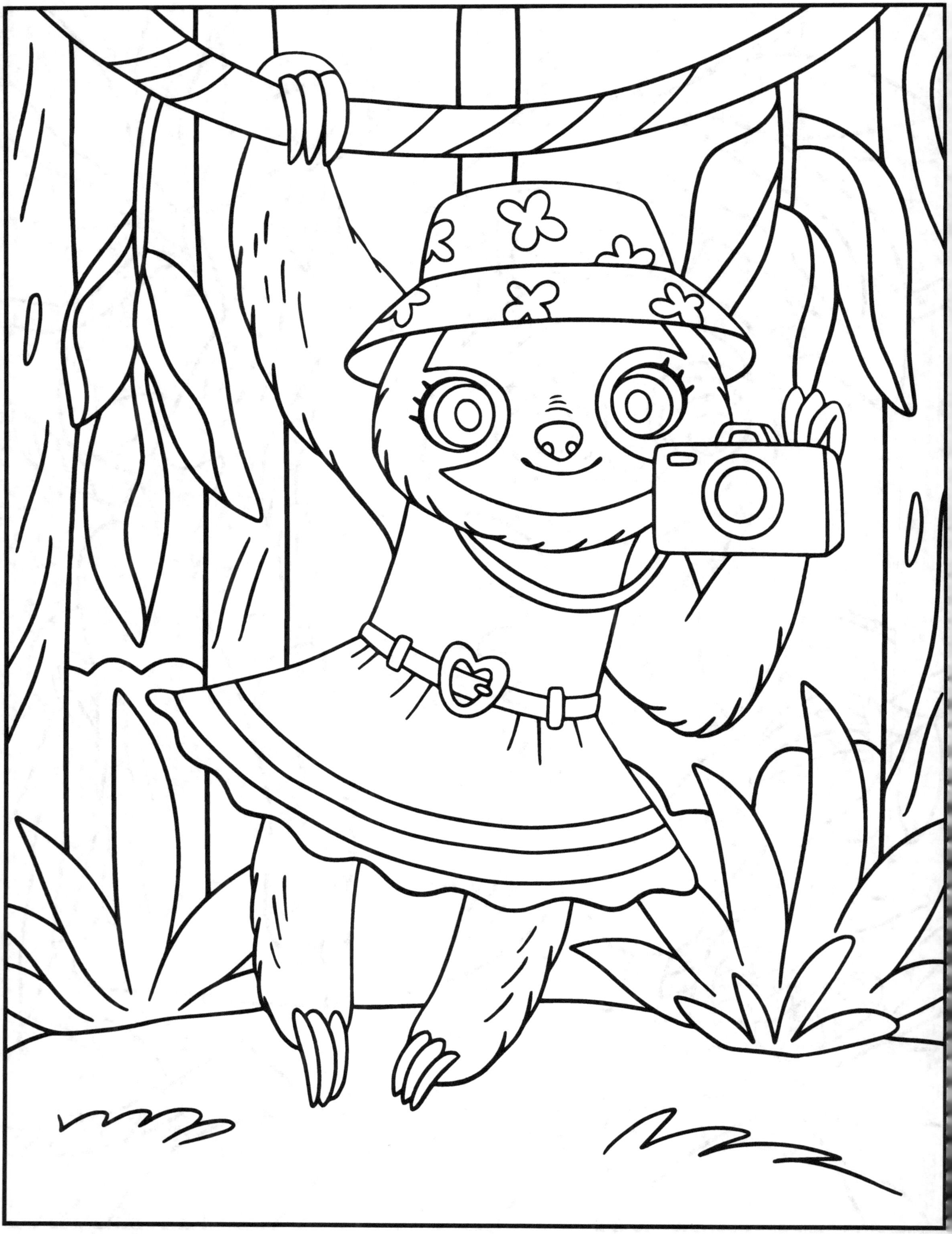

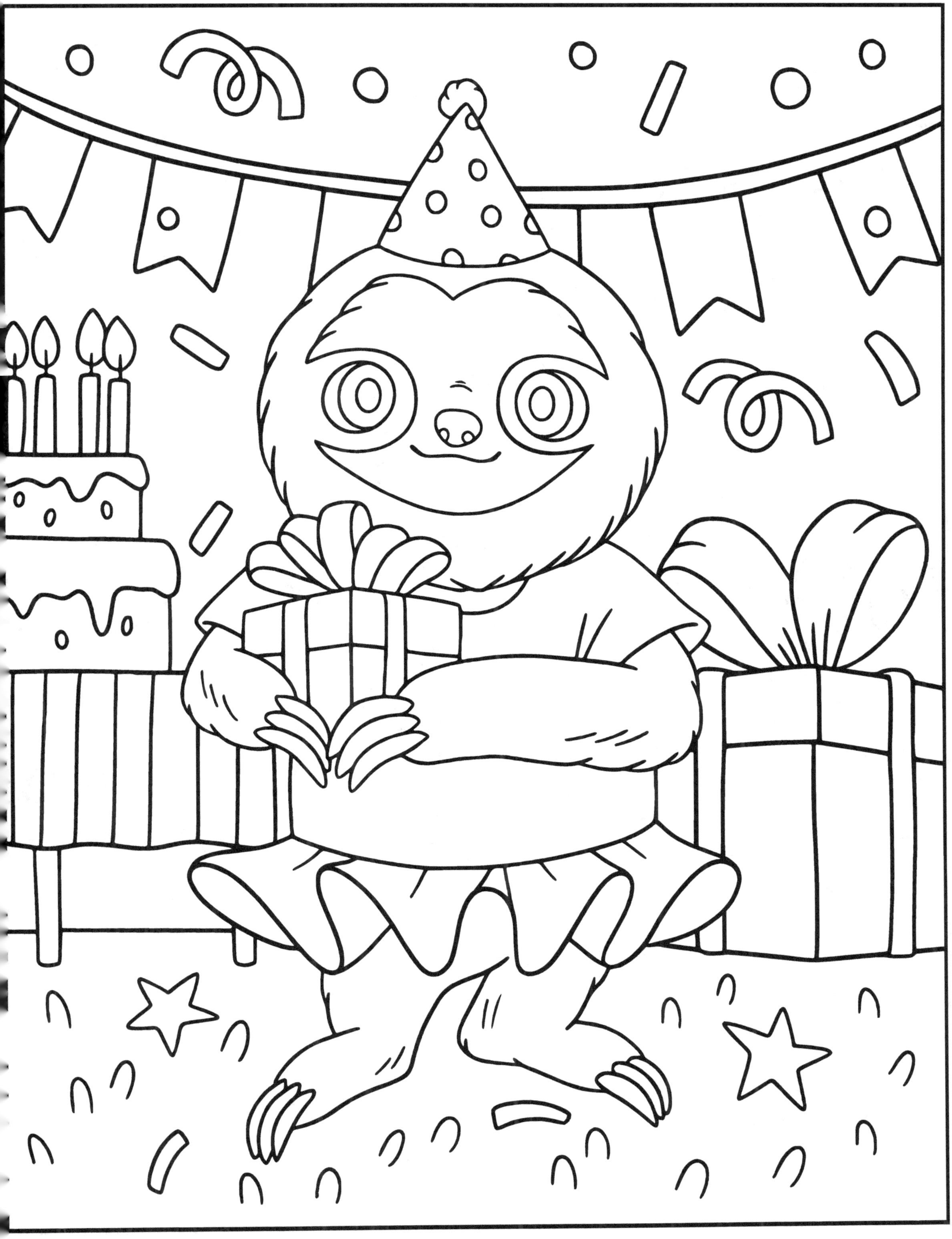

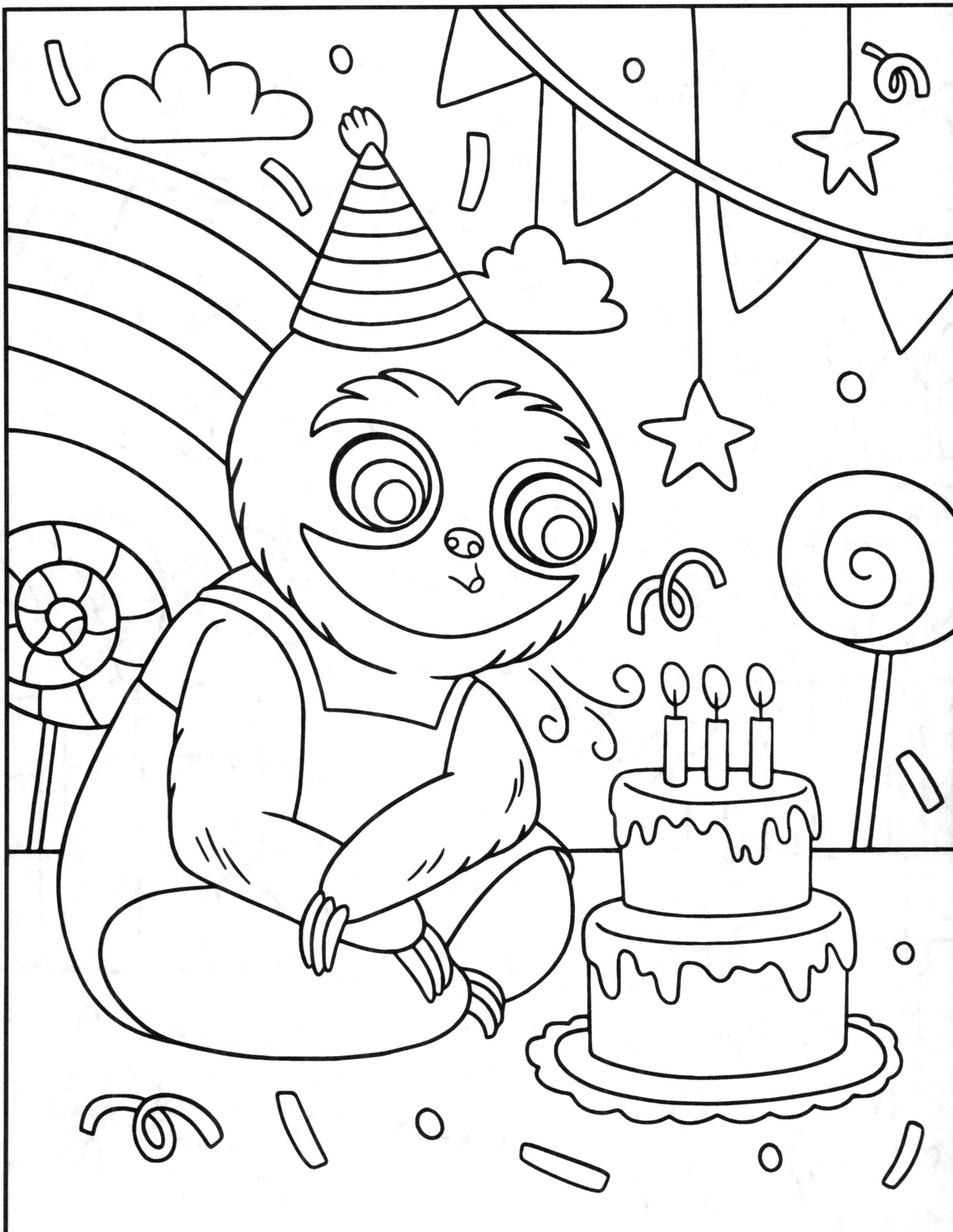

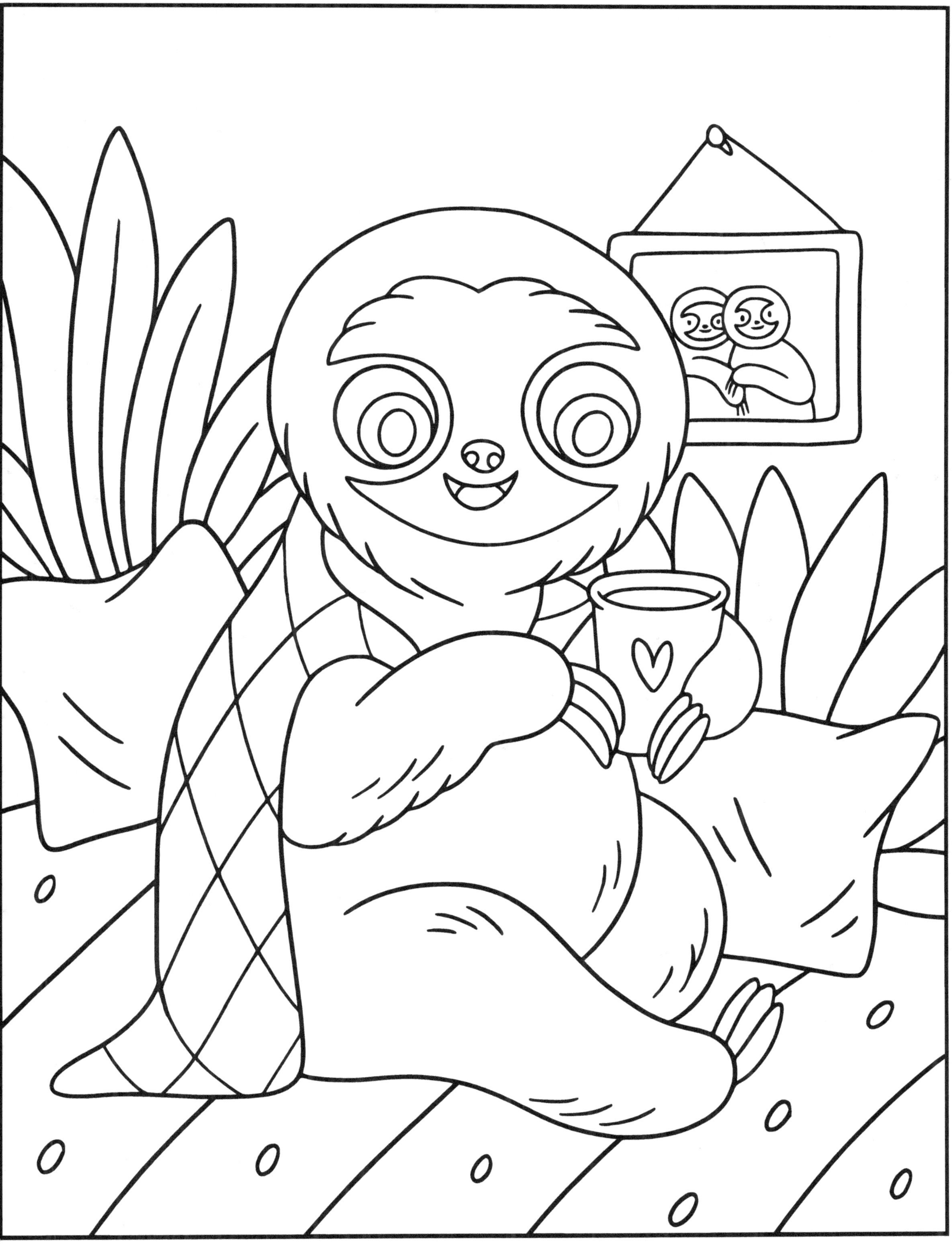

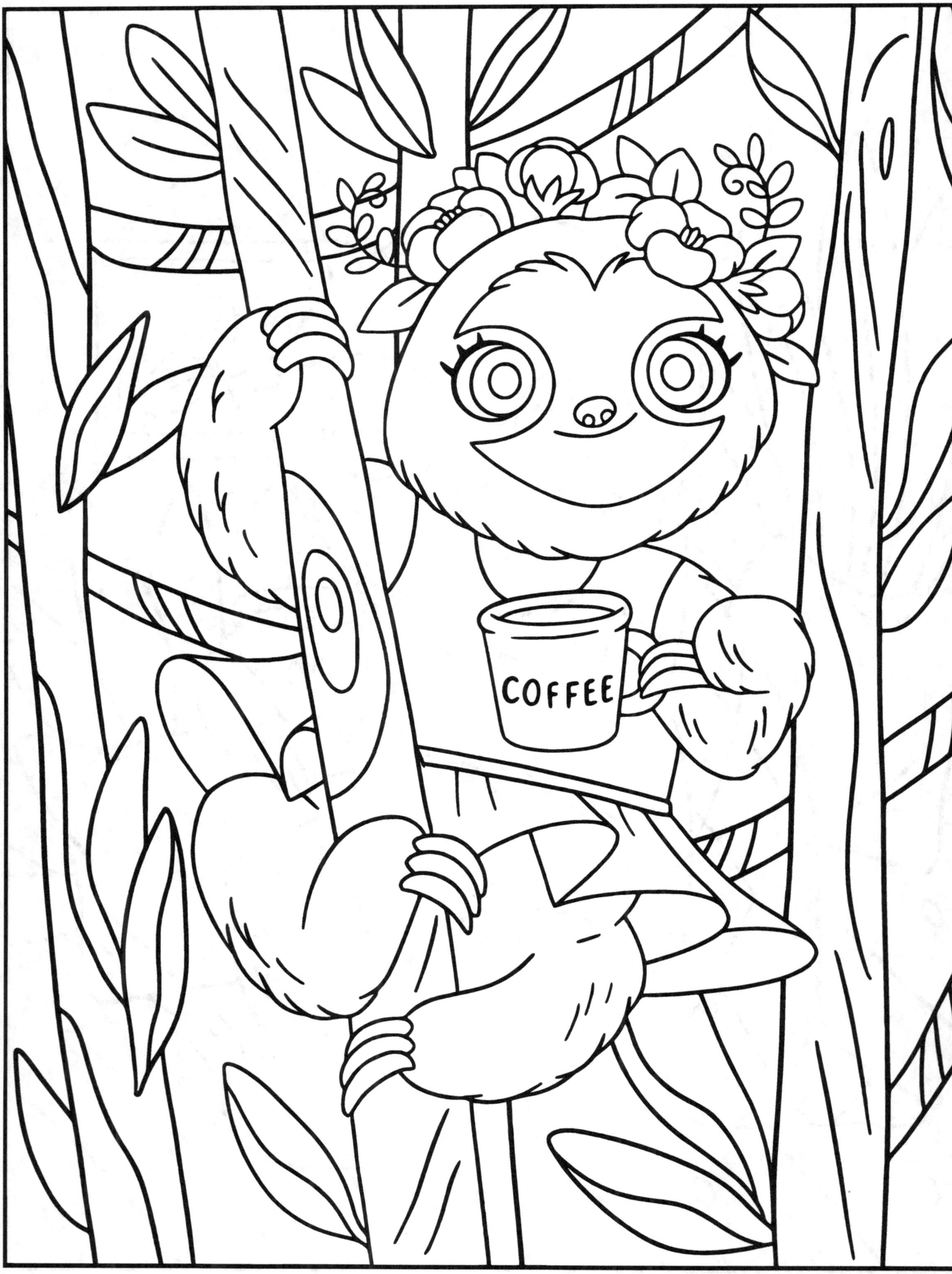
COFFEE

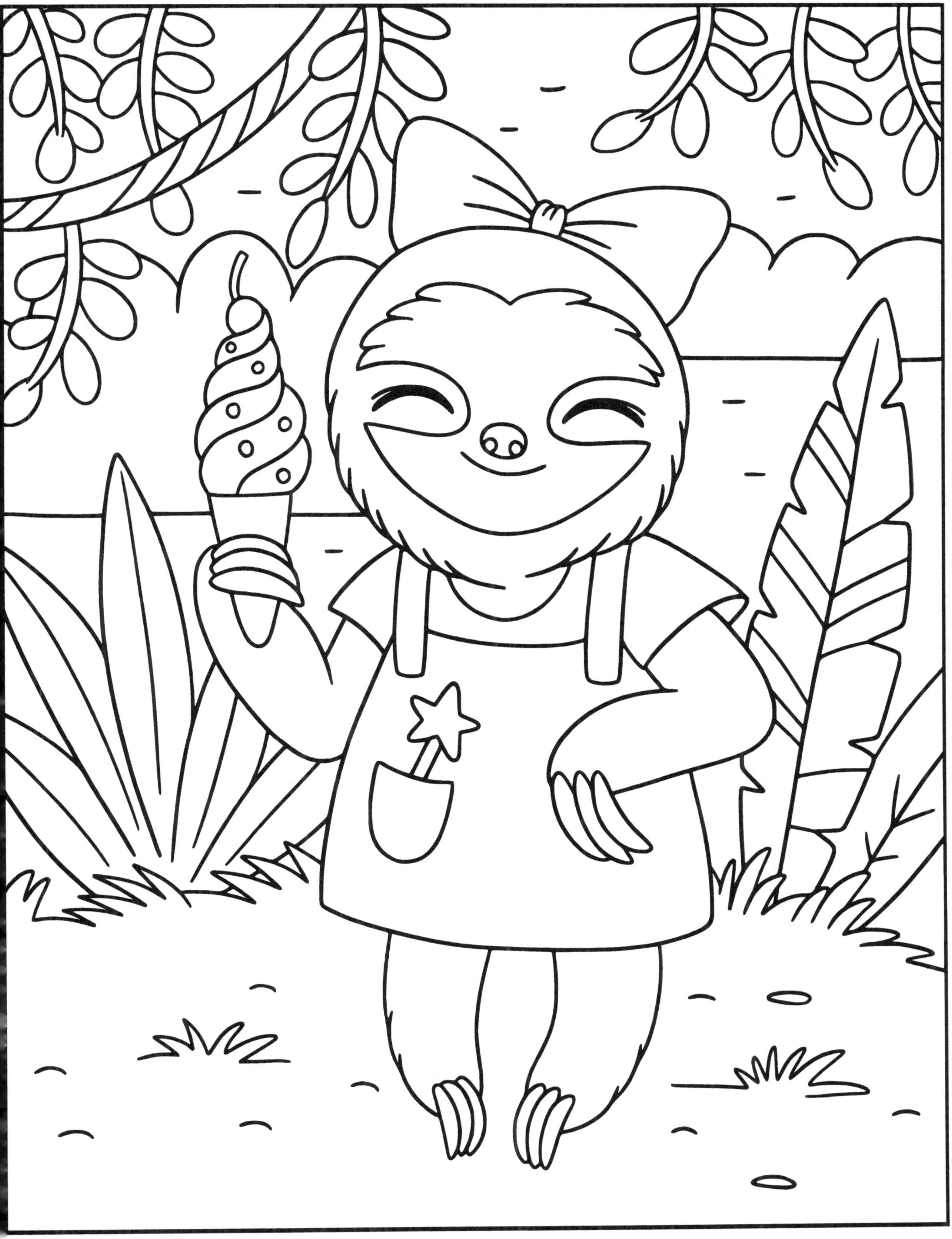

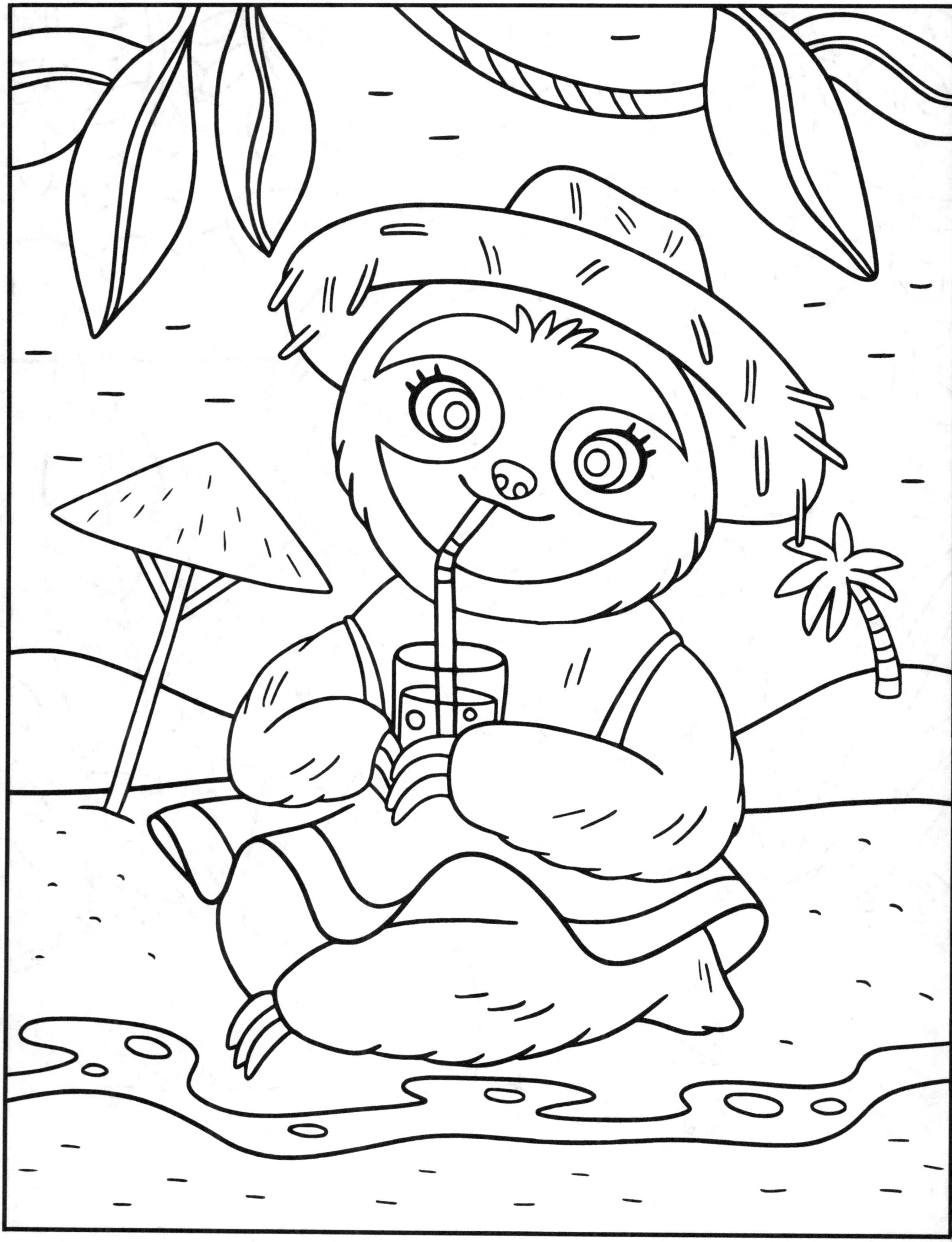

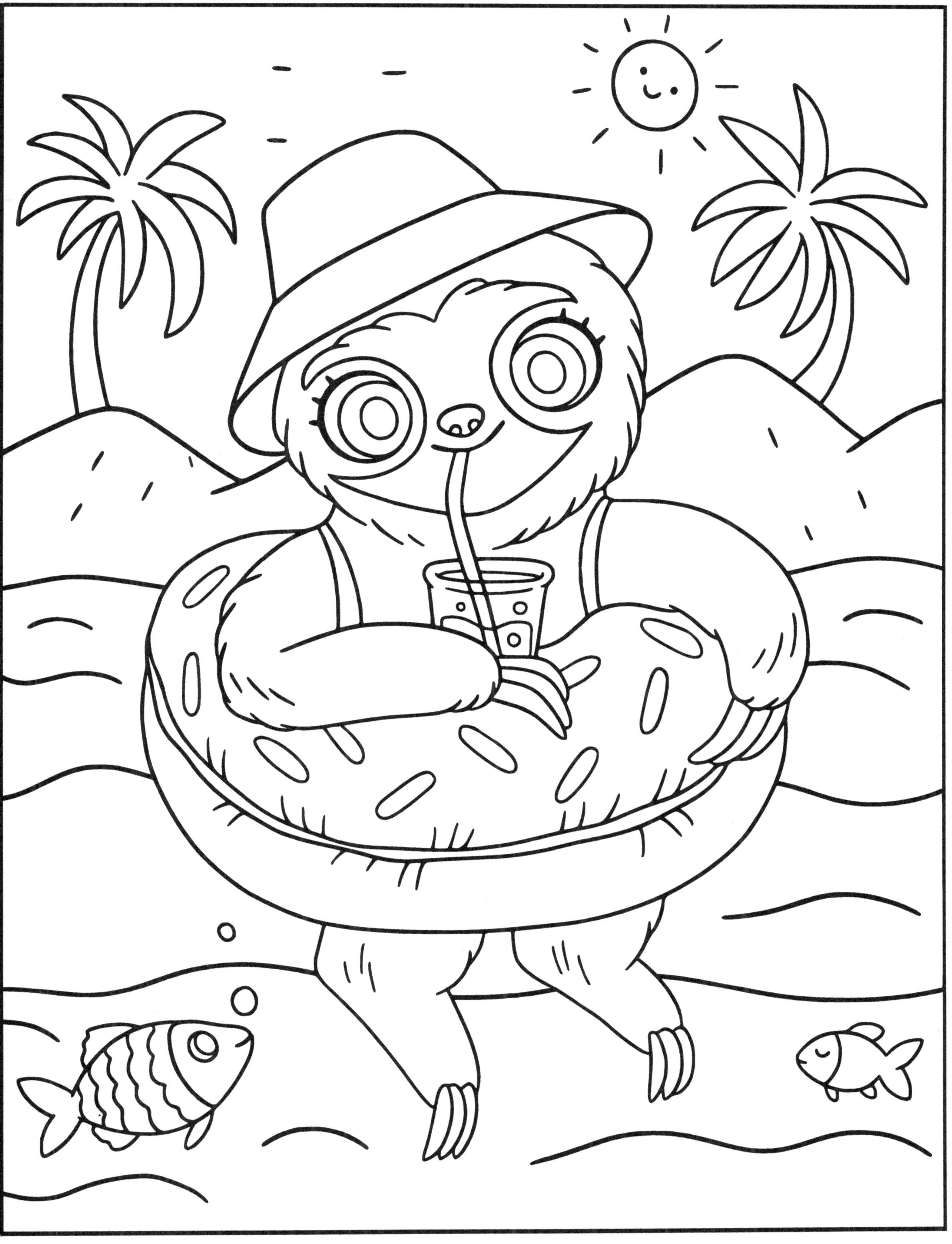

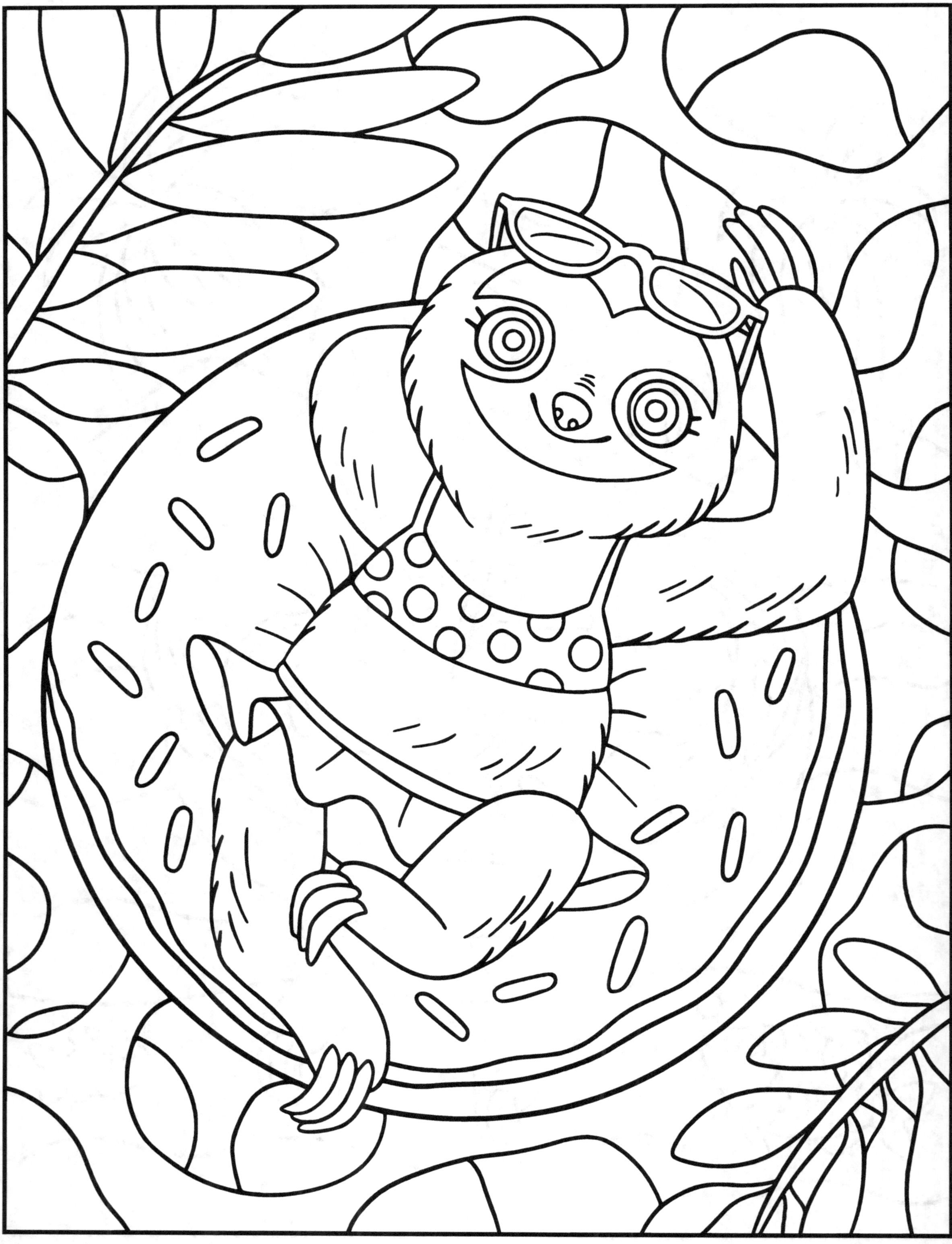

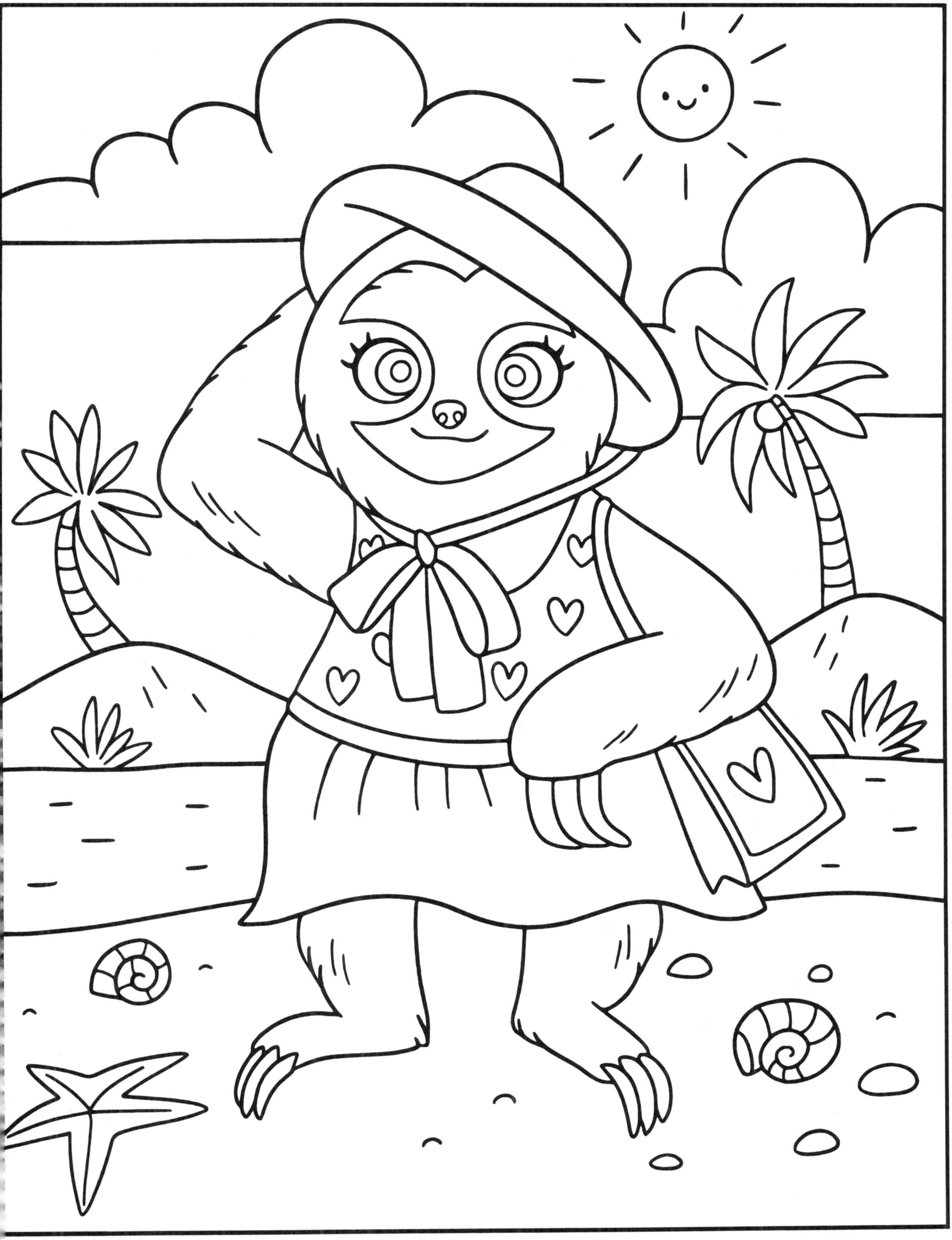

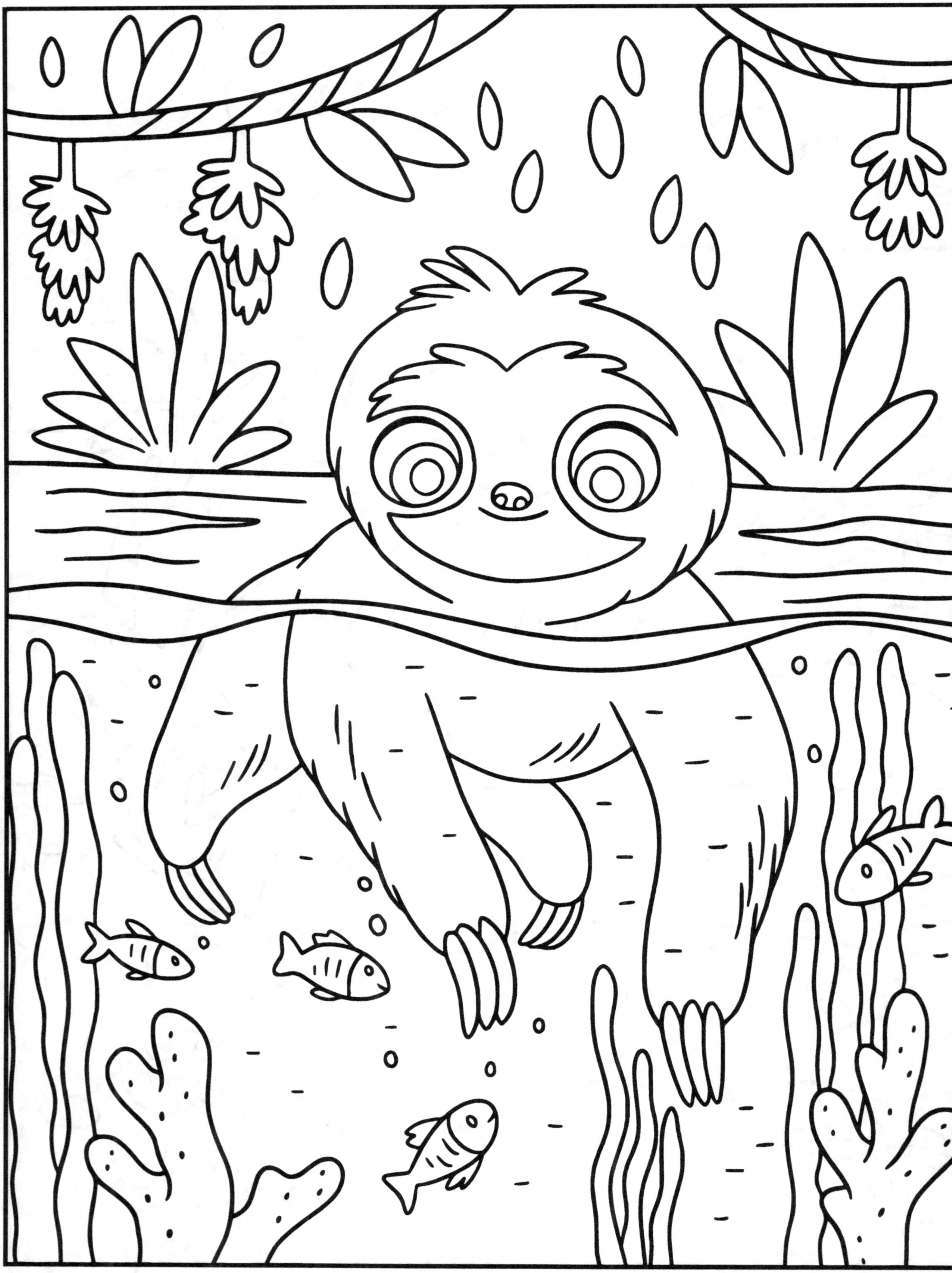

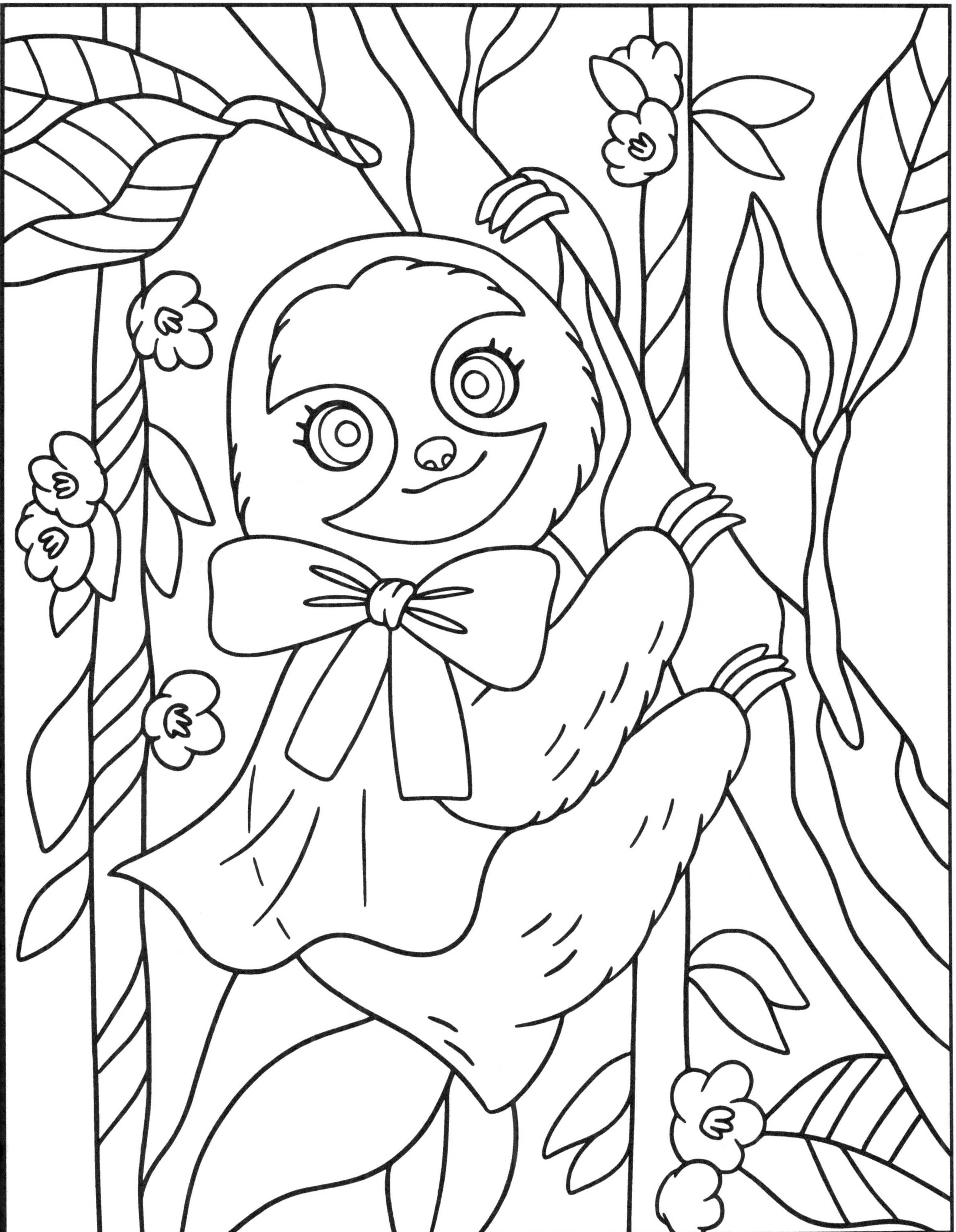

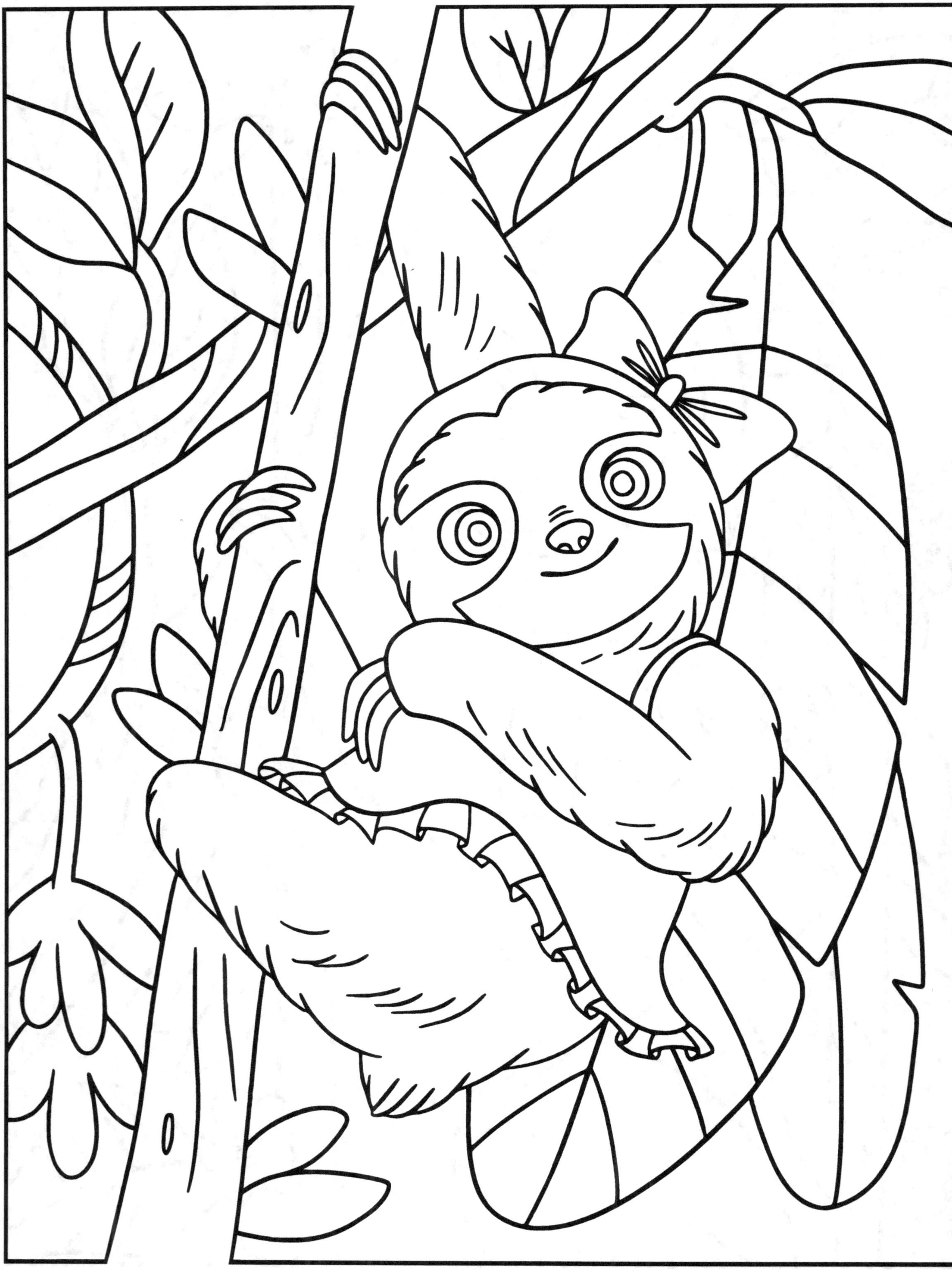

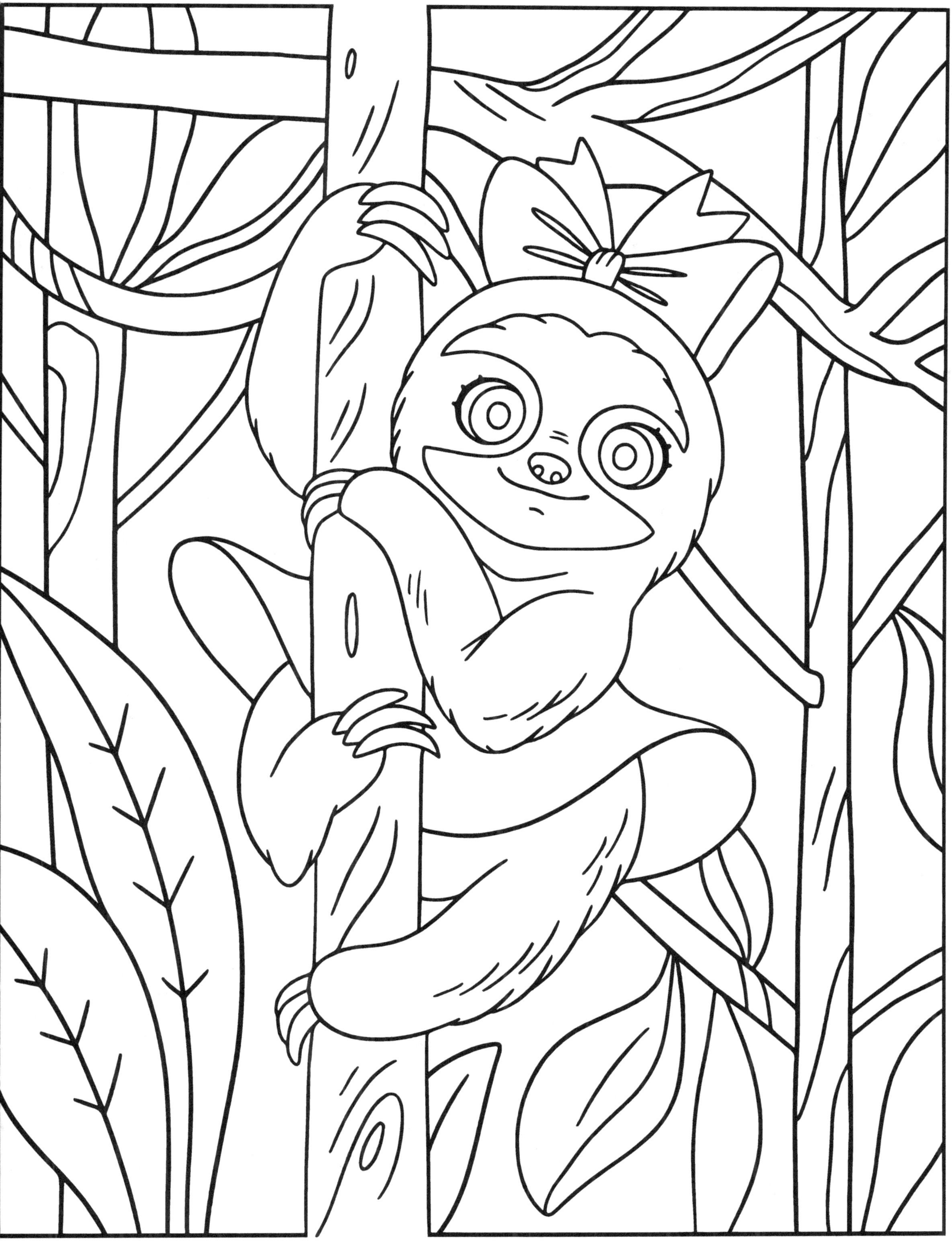

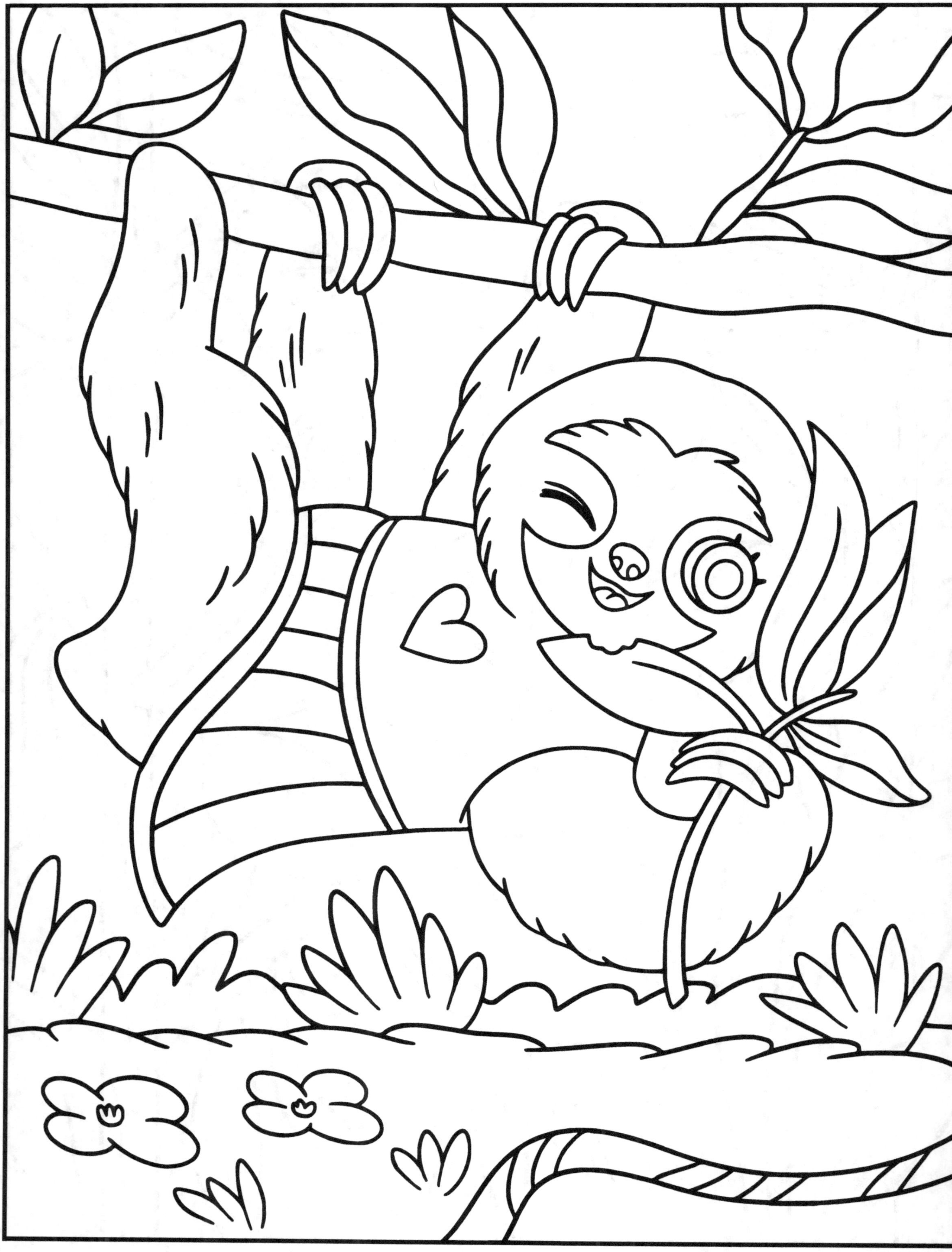

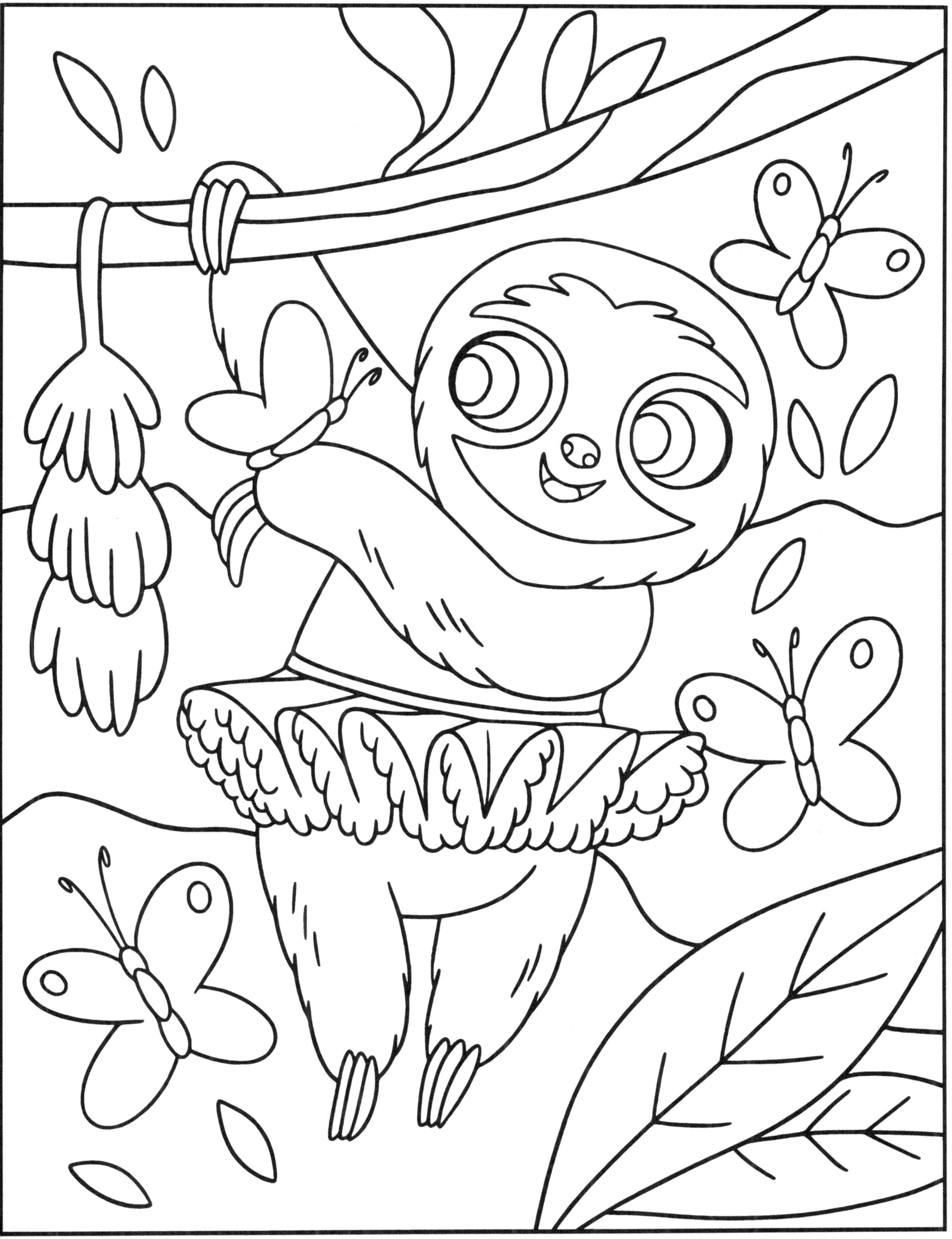

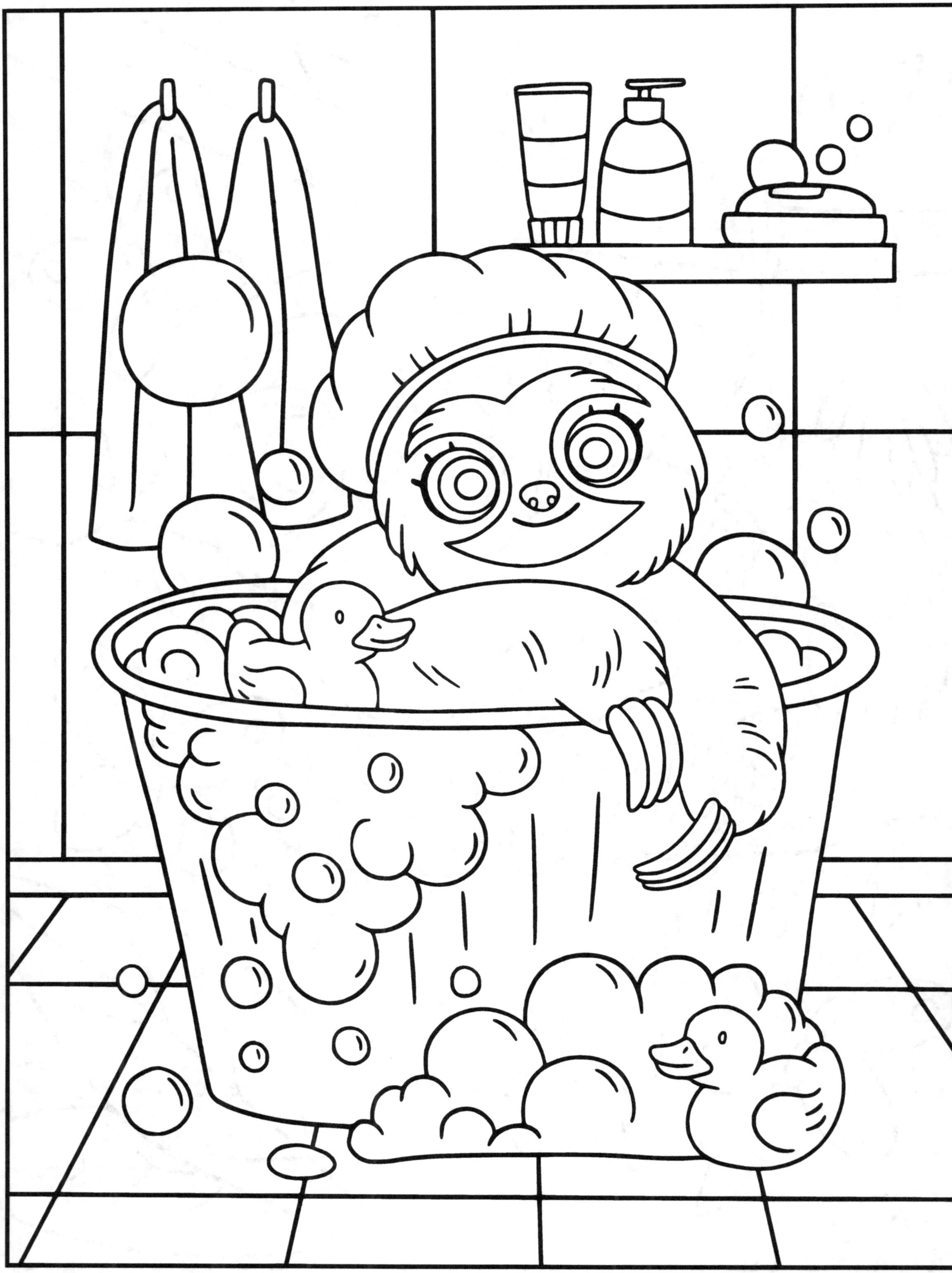

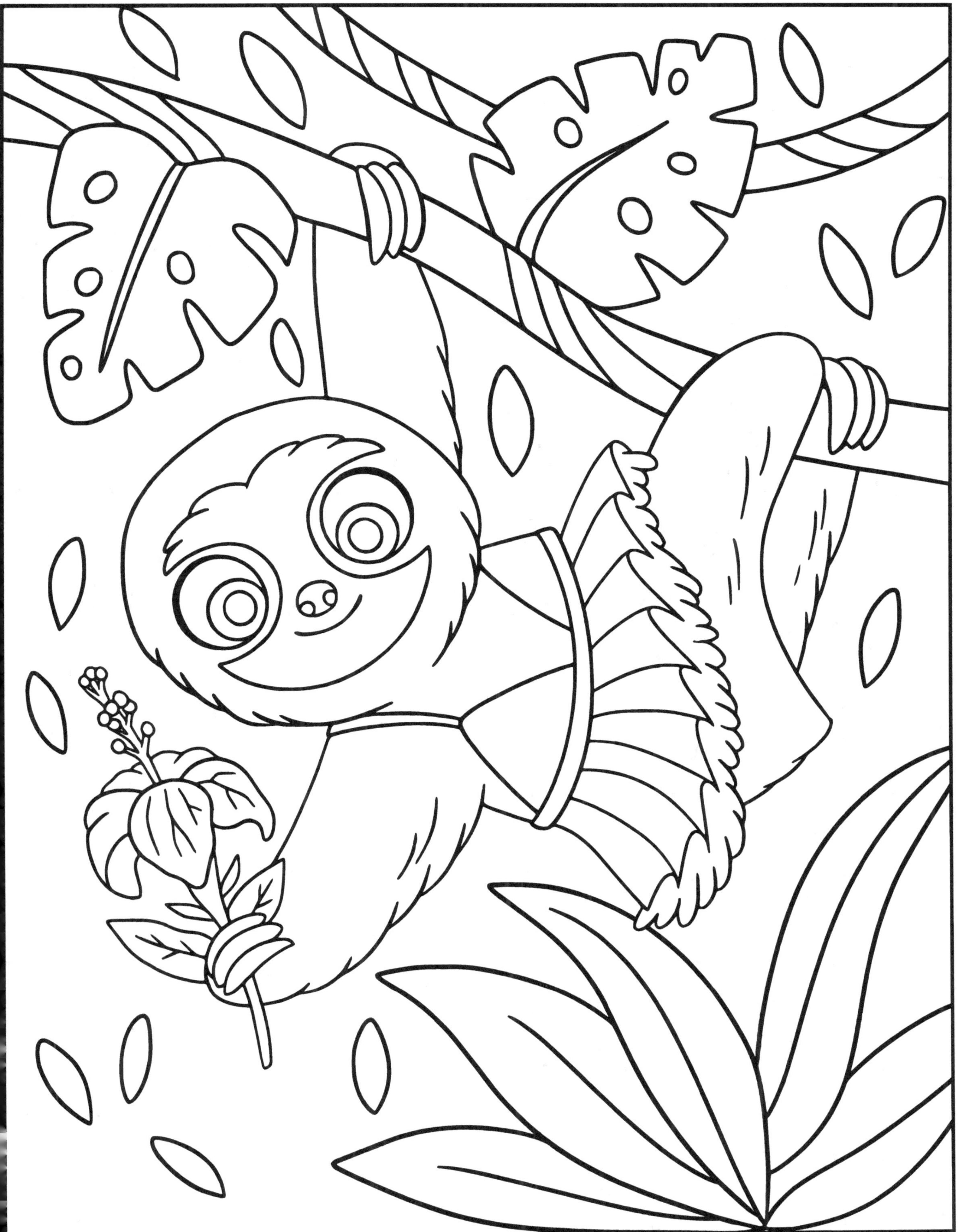

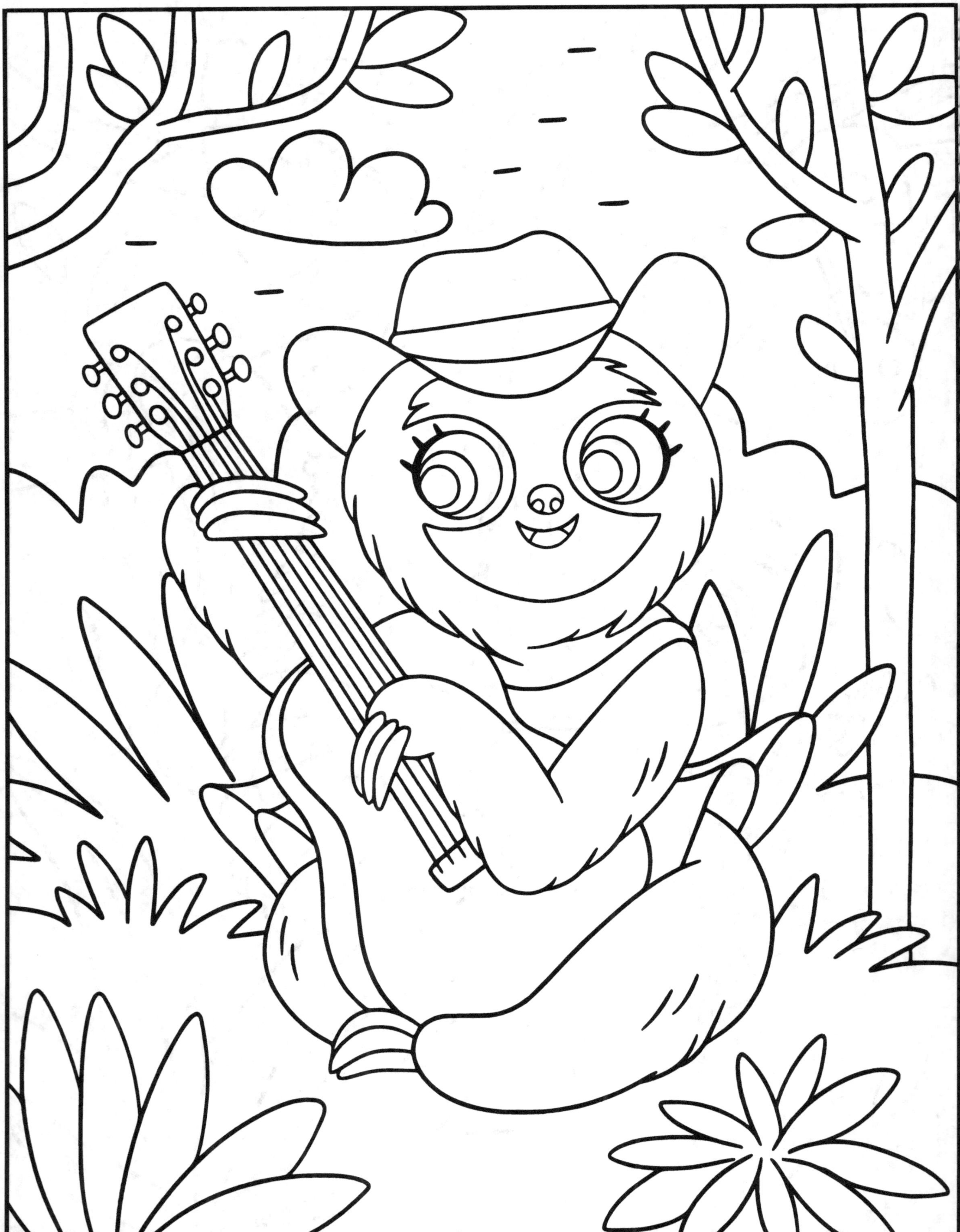

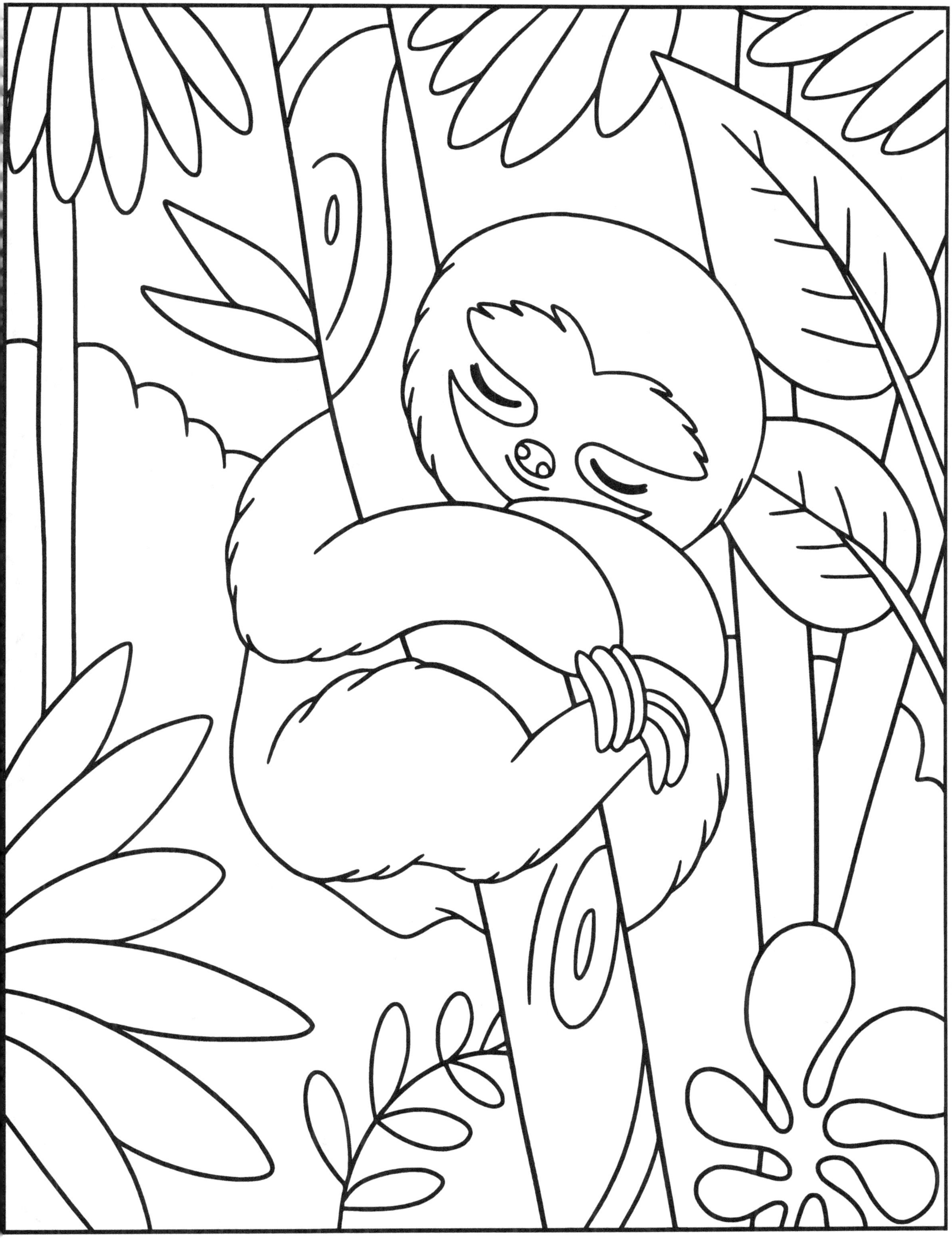

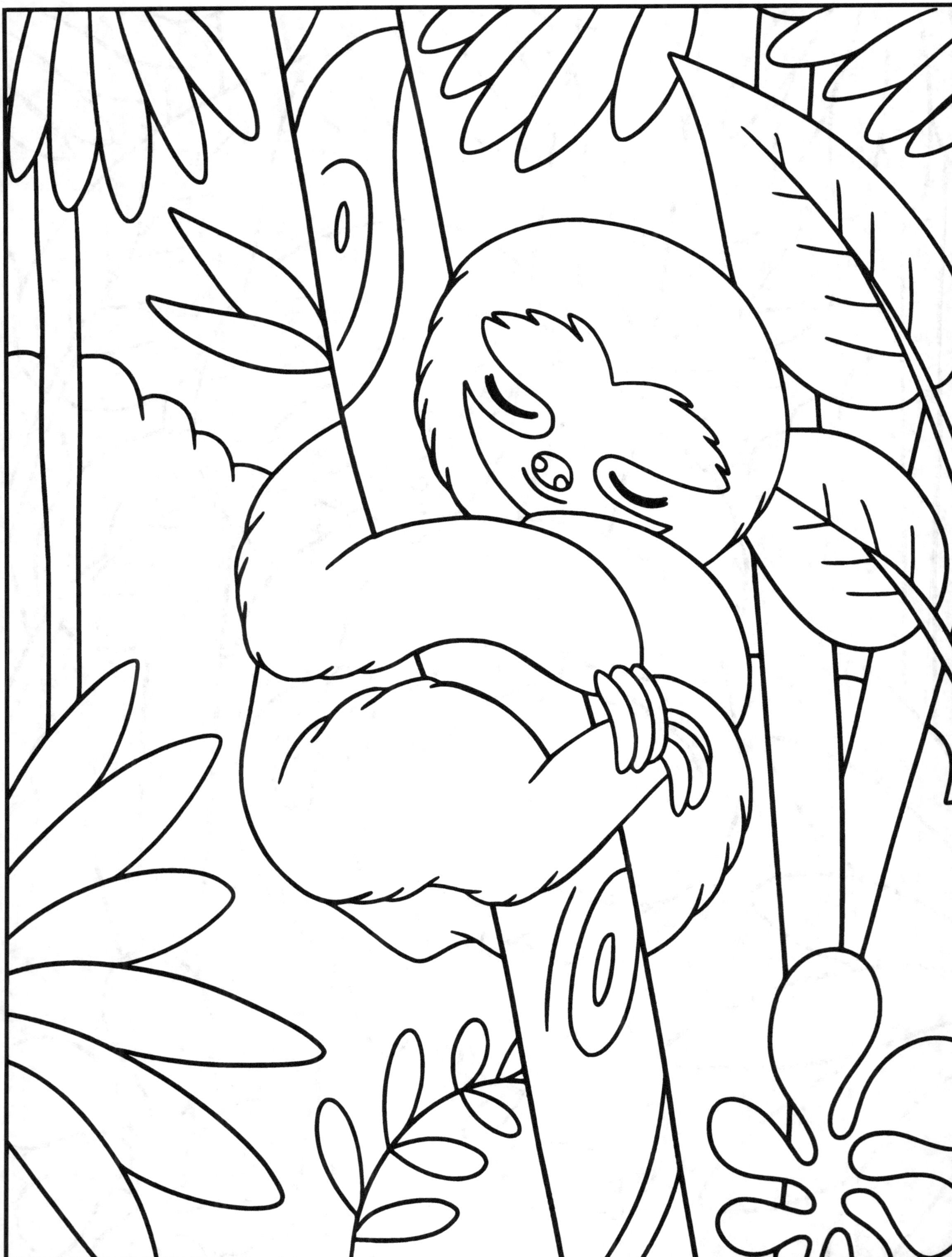

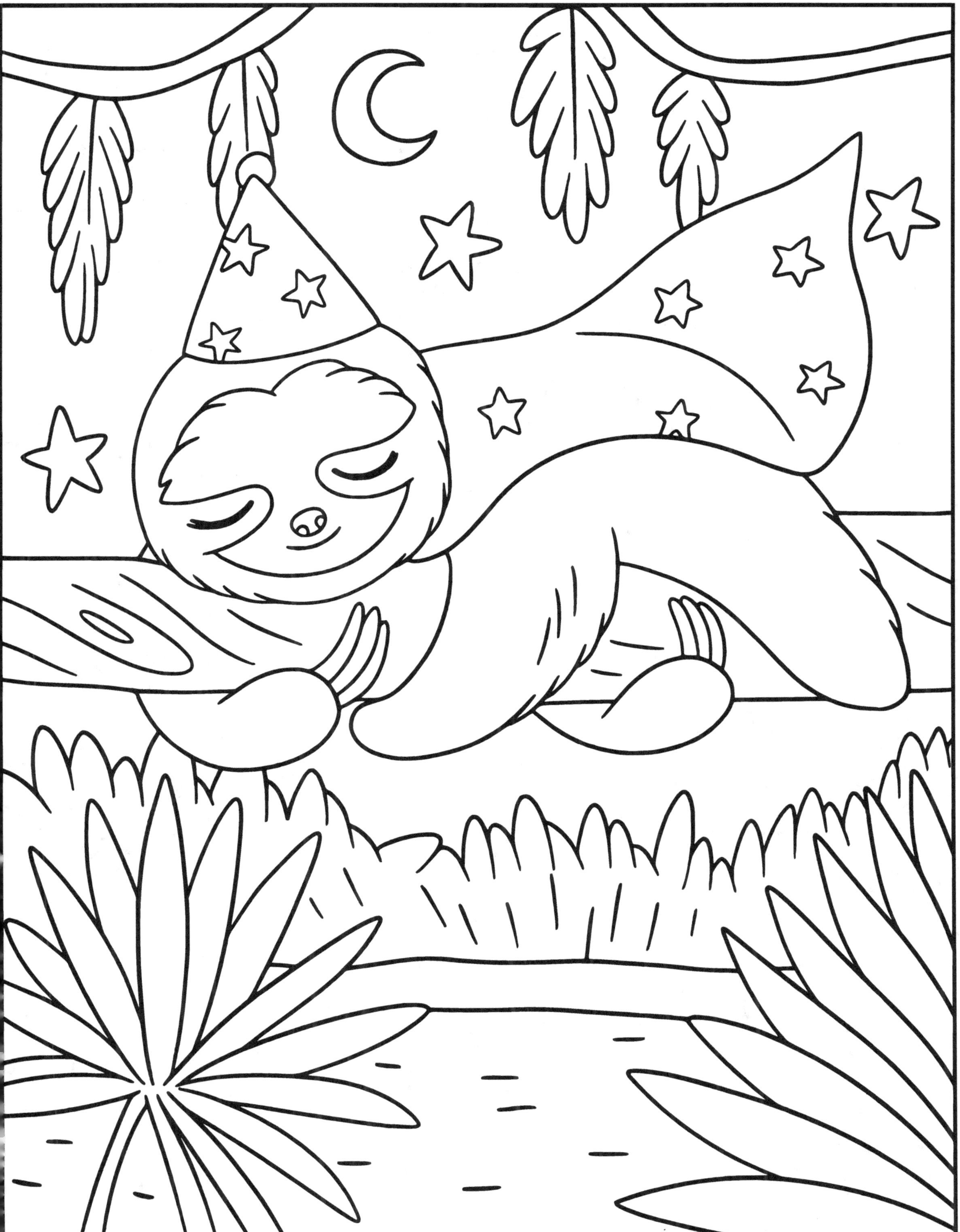

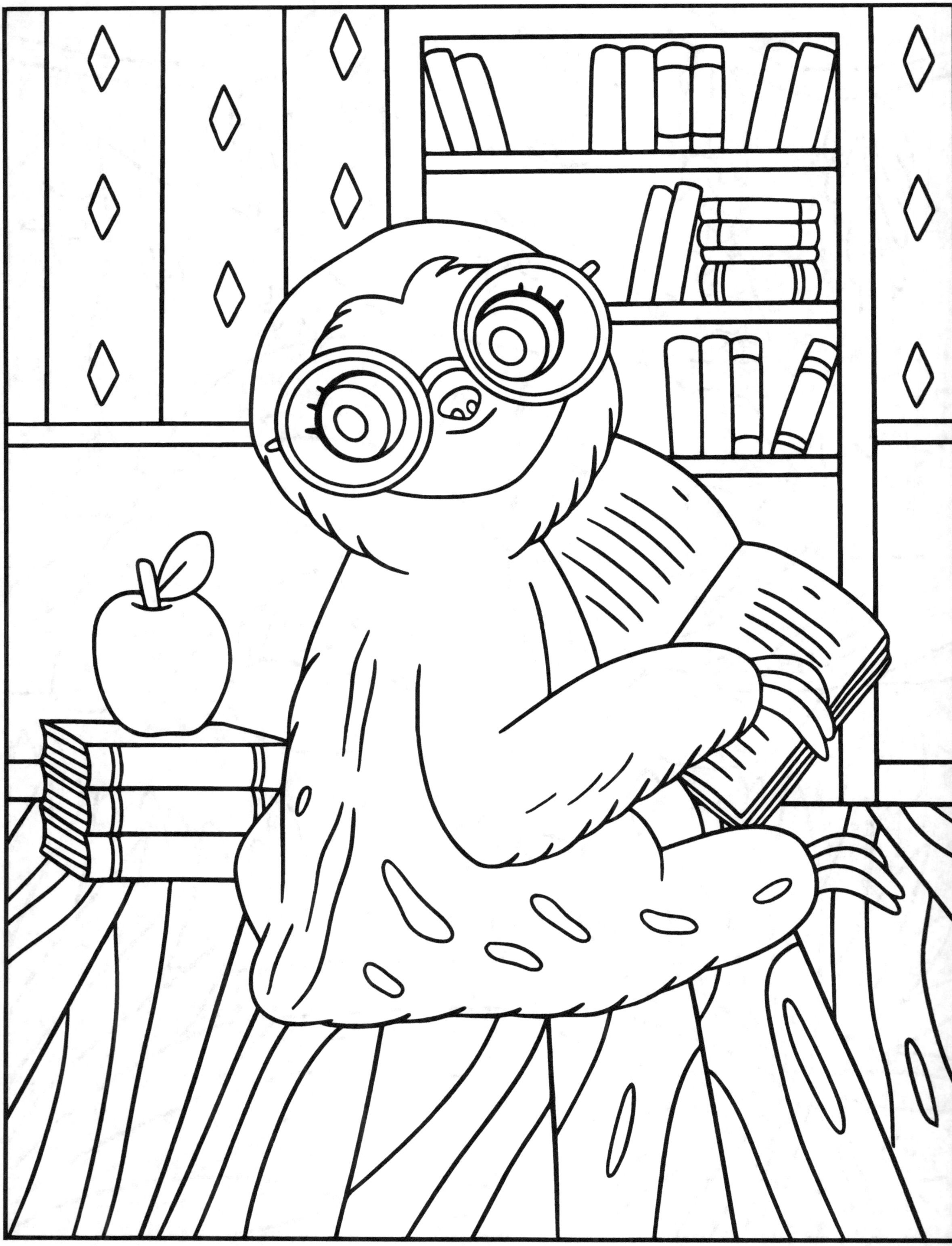

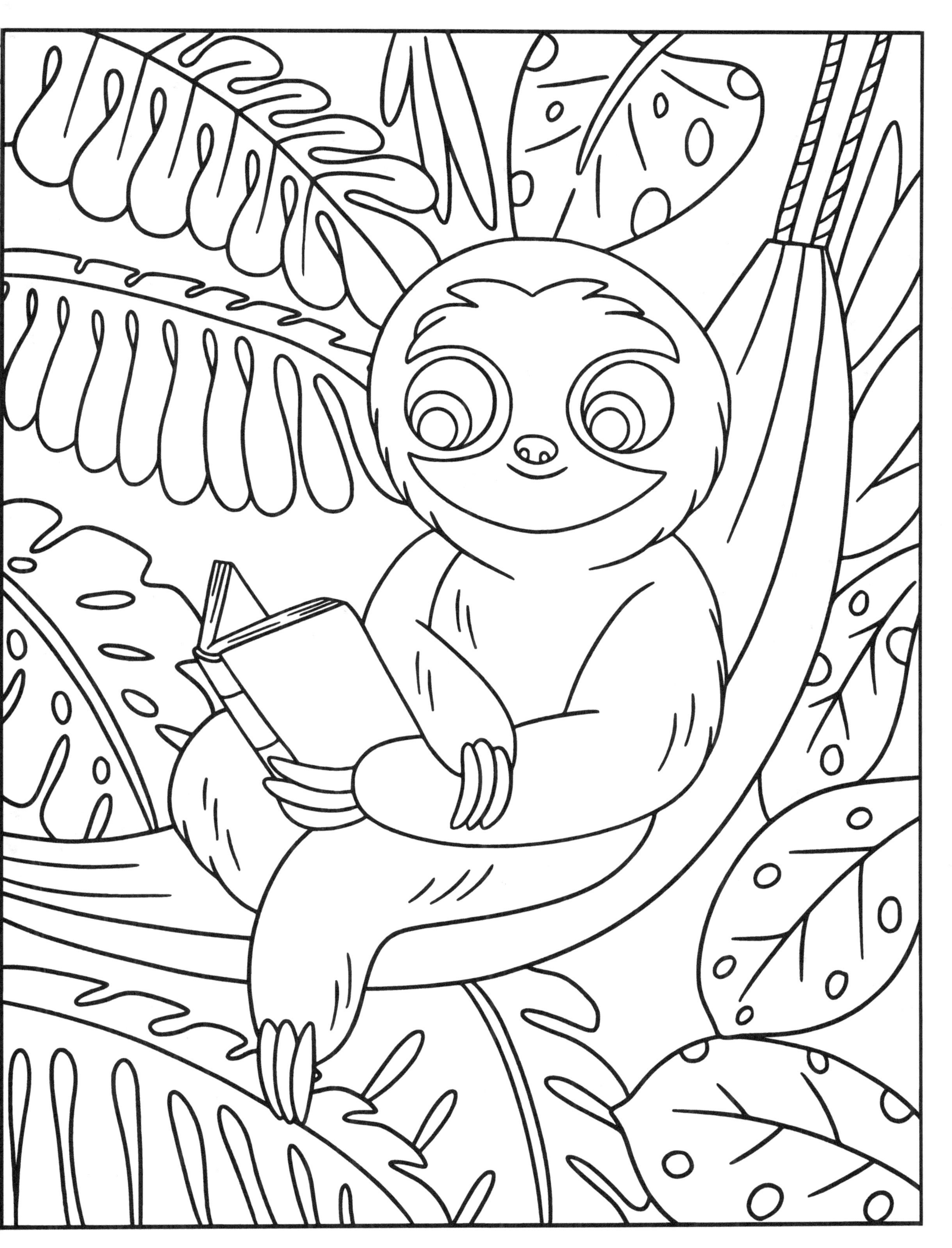

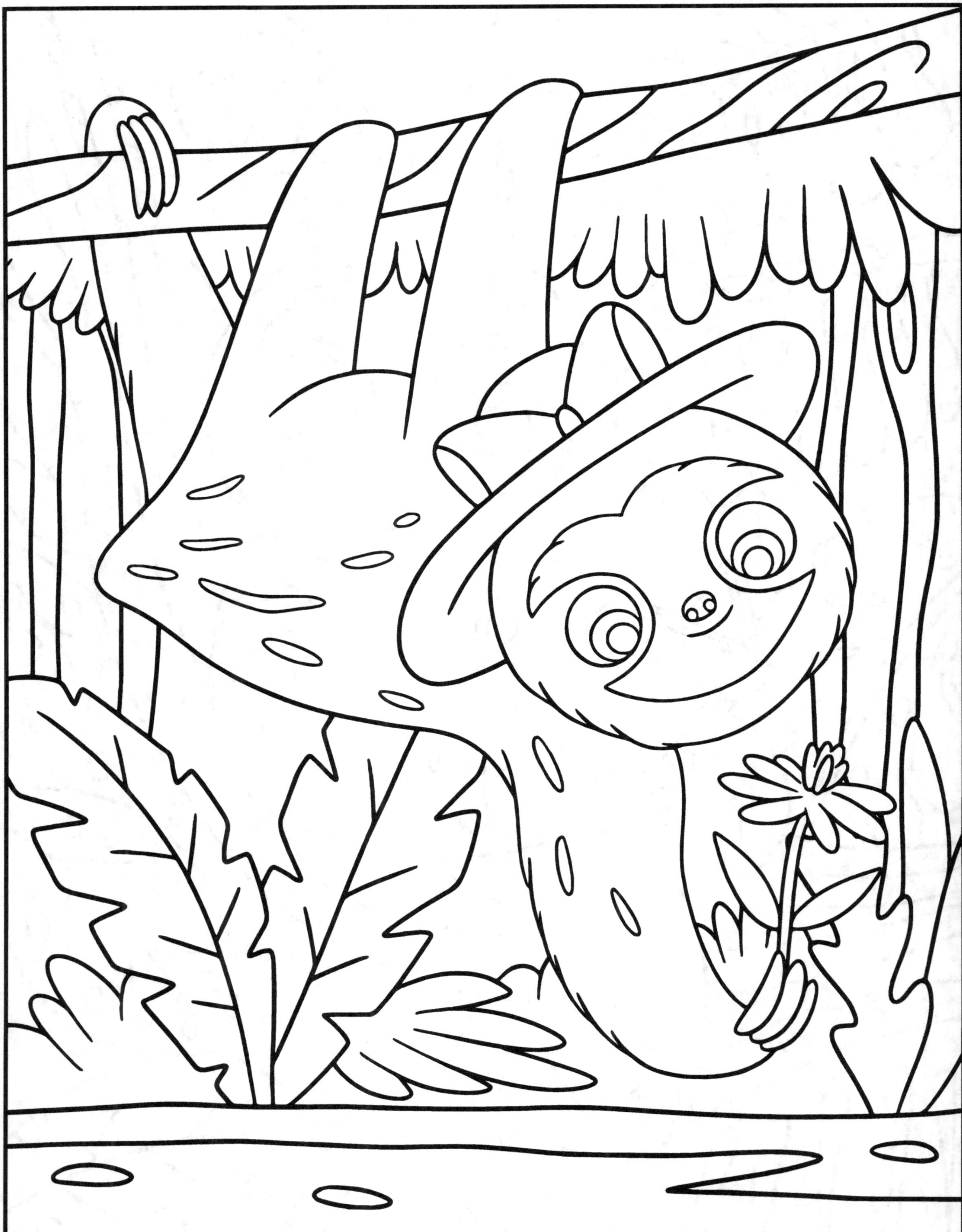

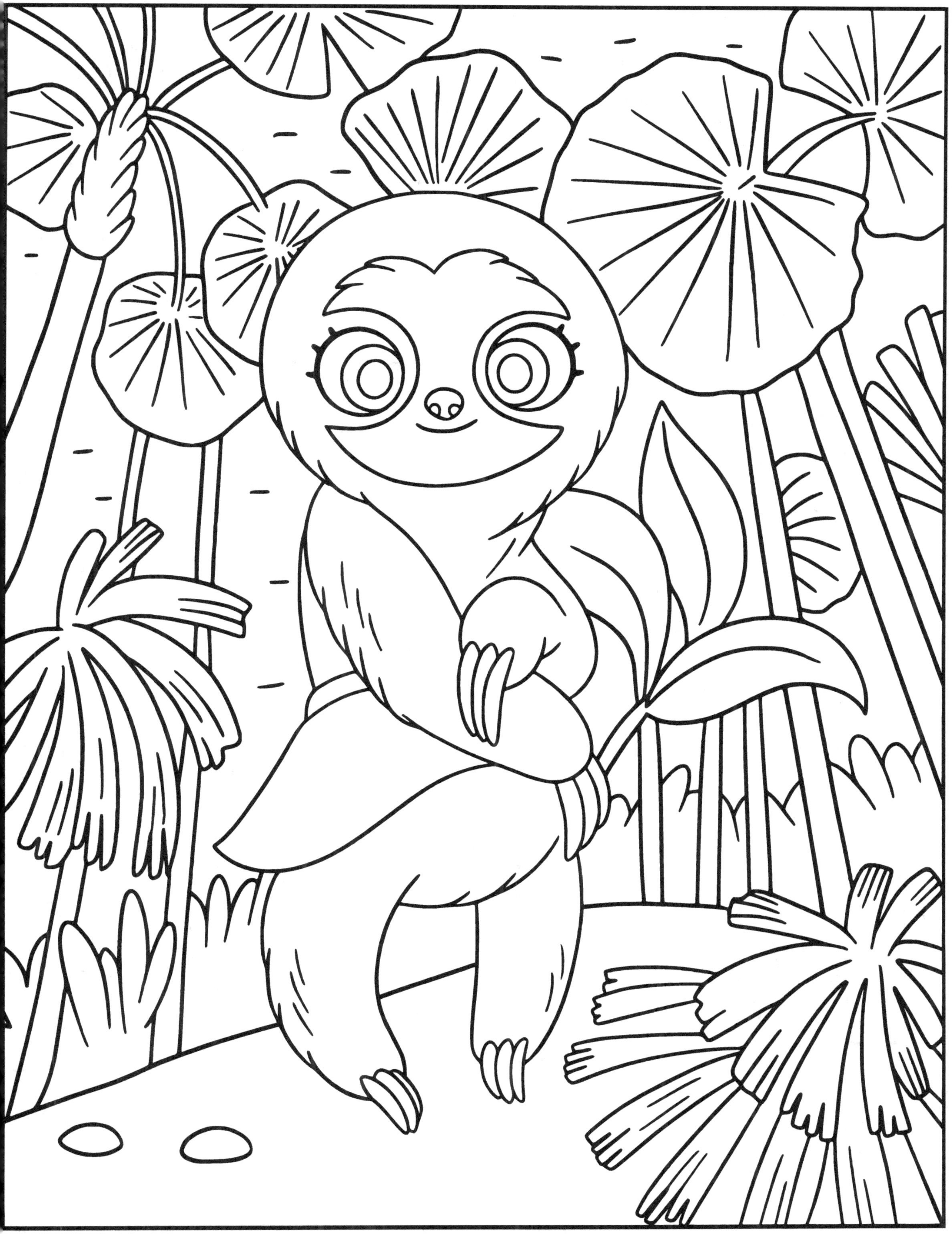

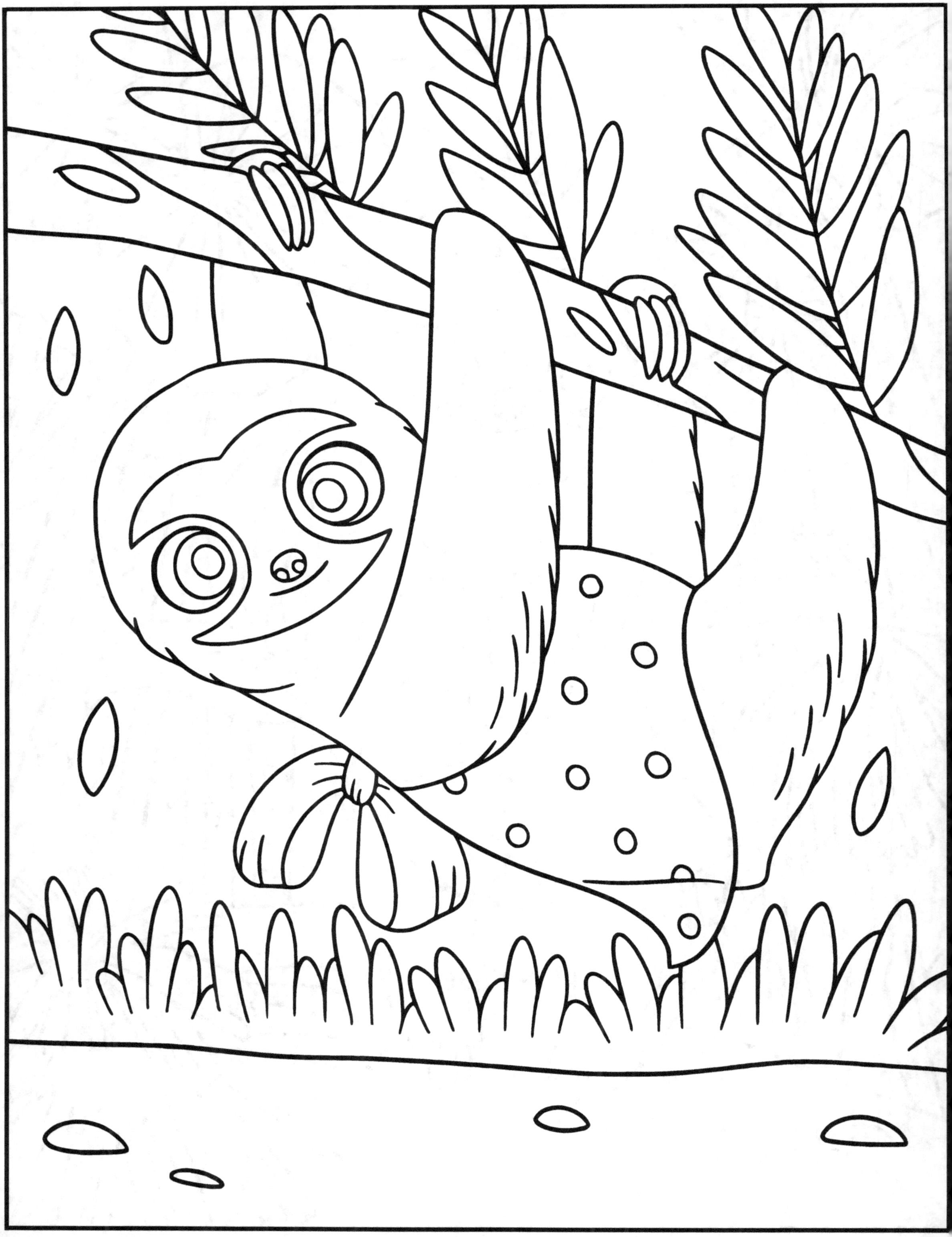

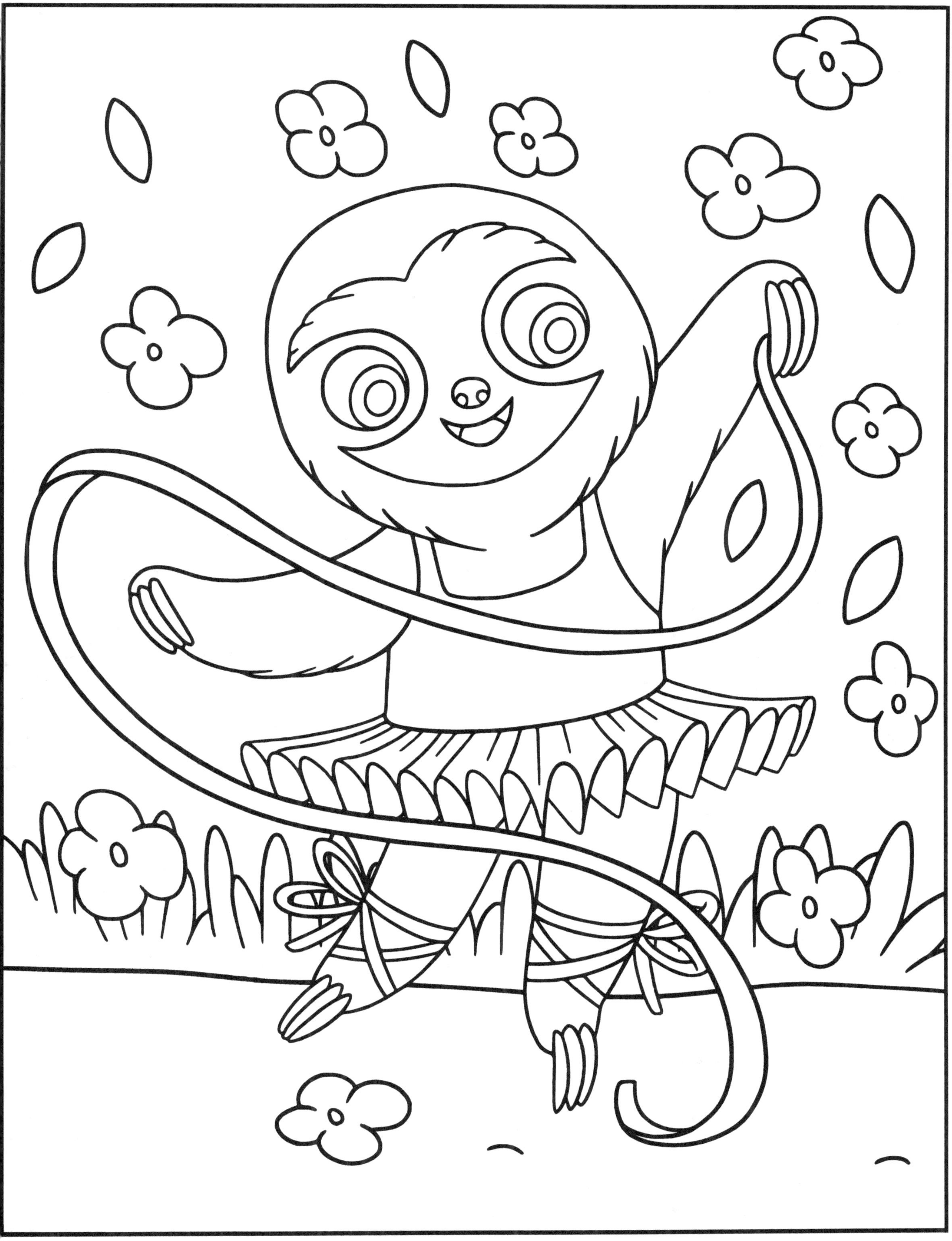

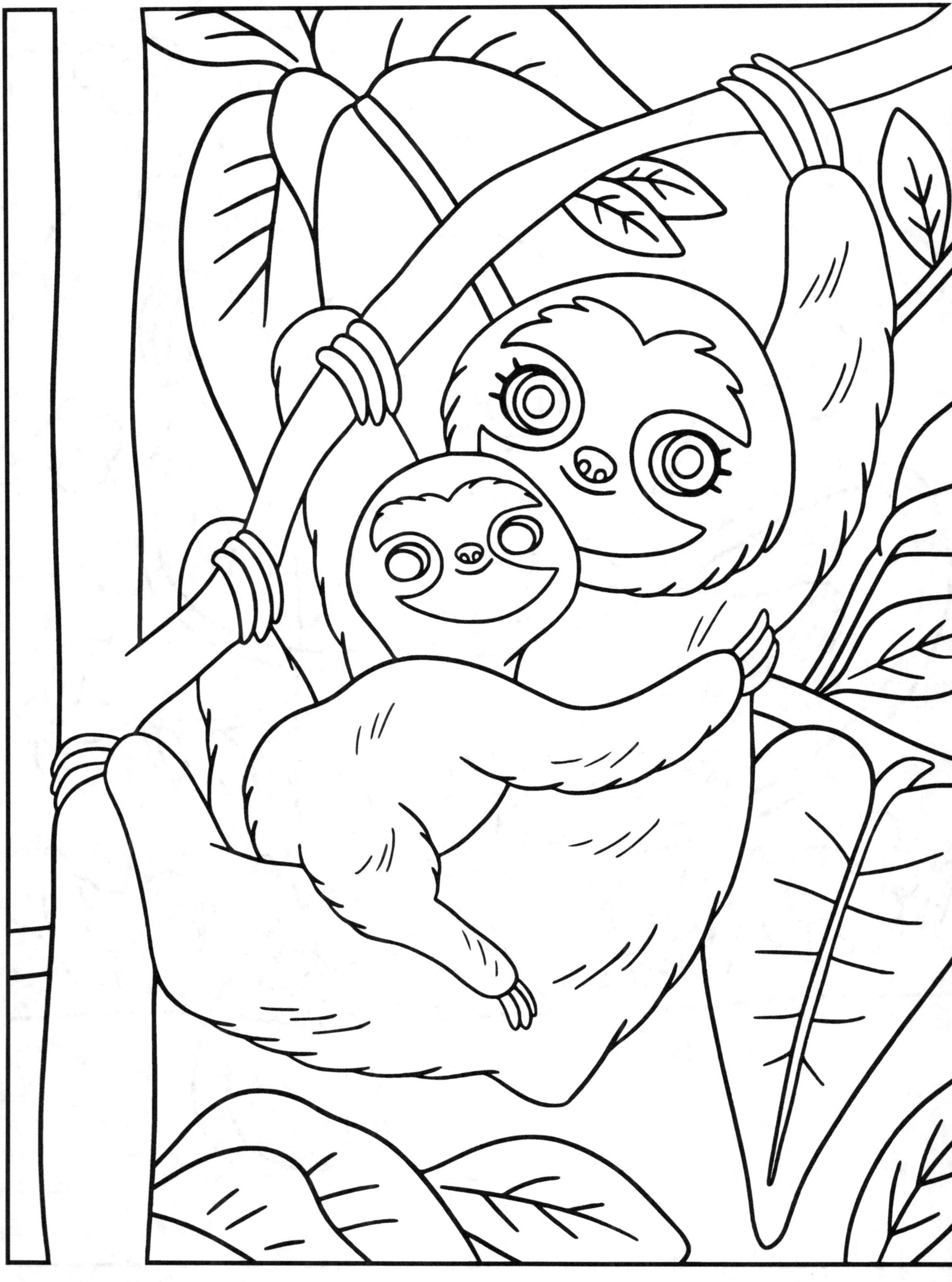

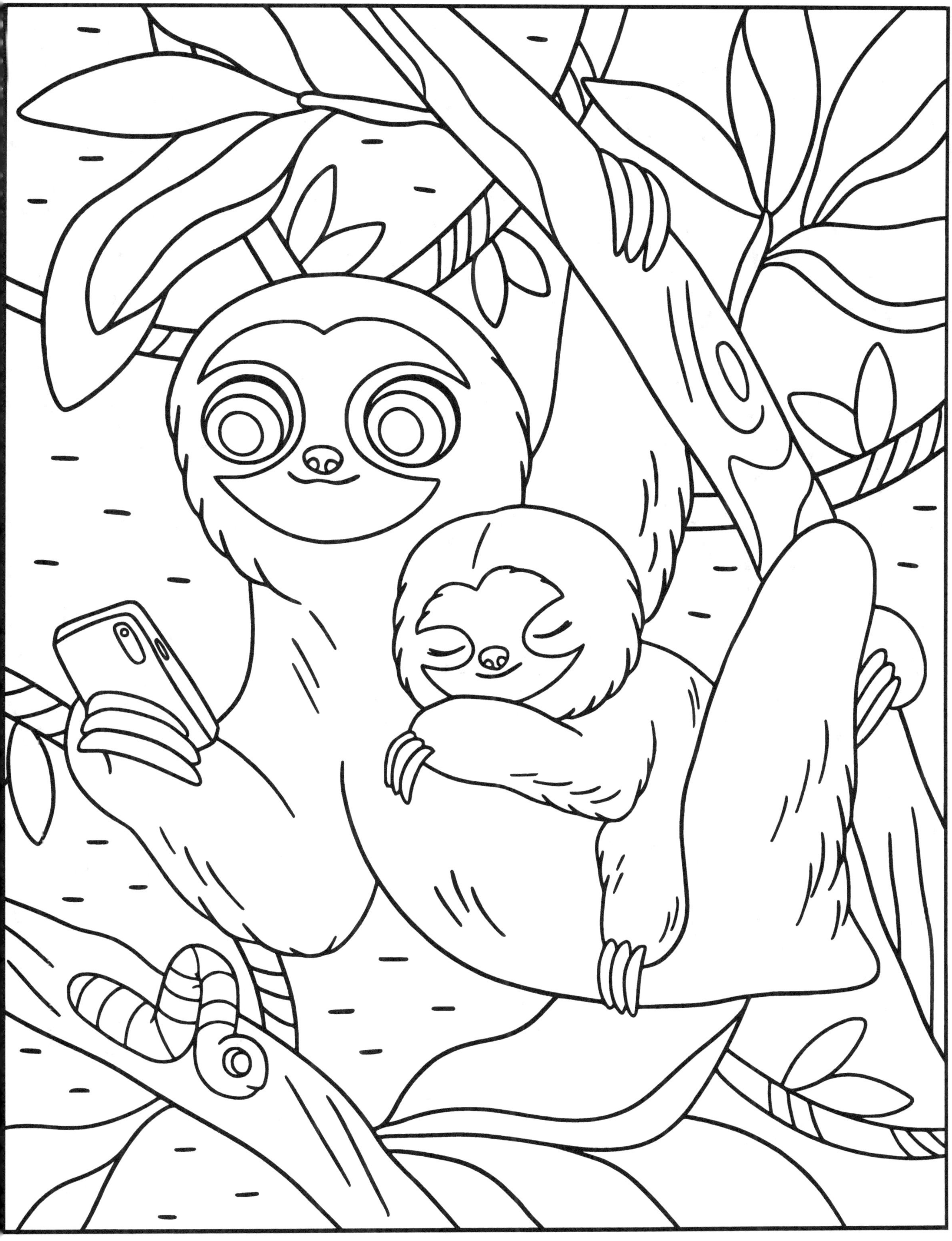

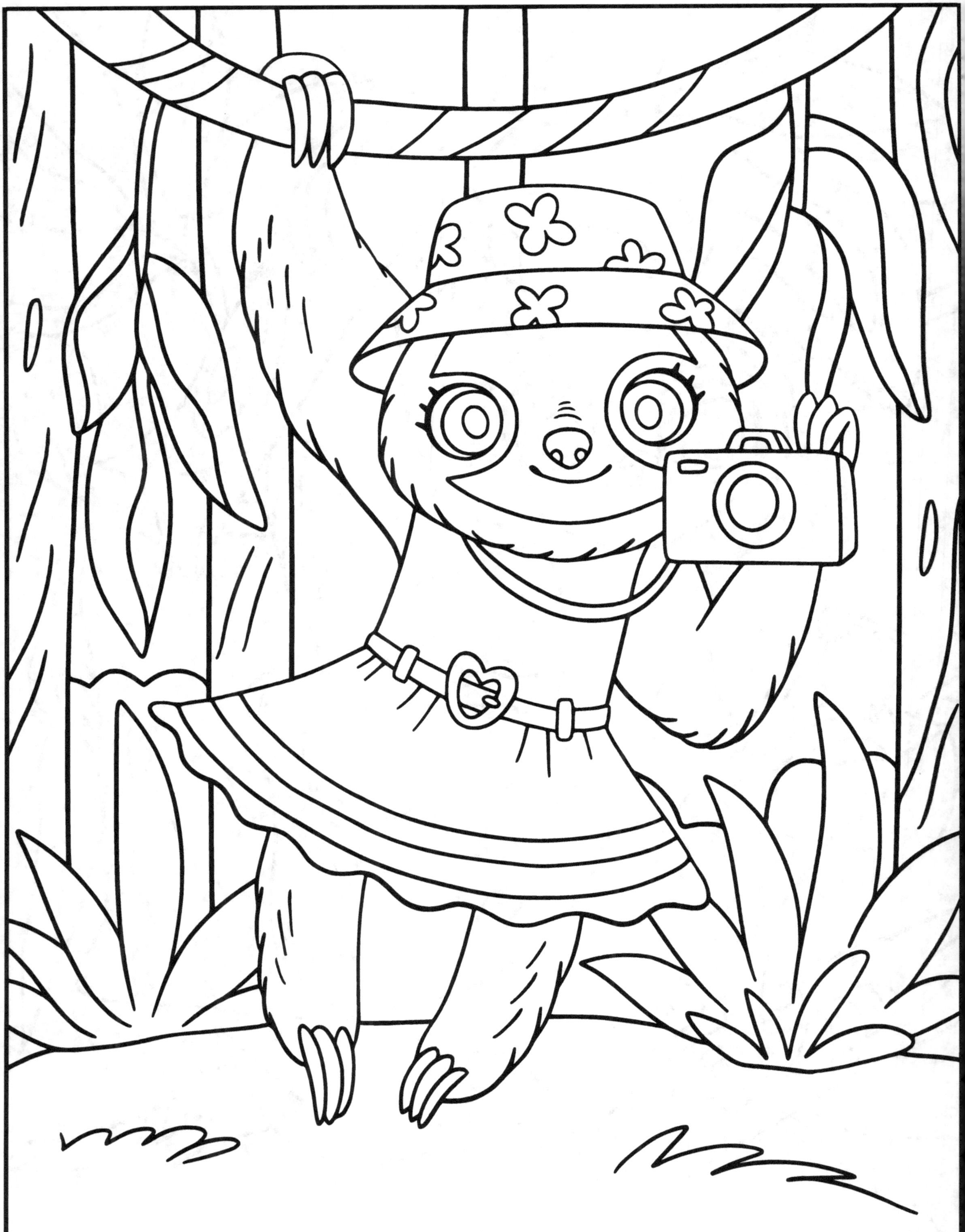

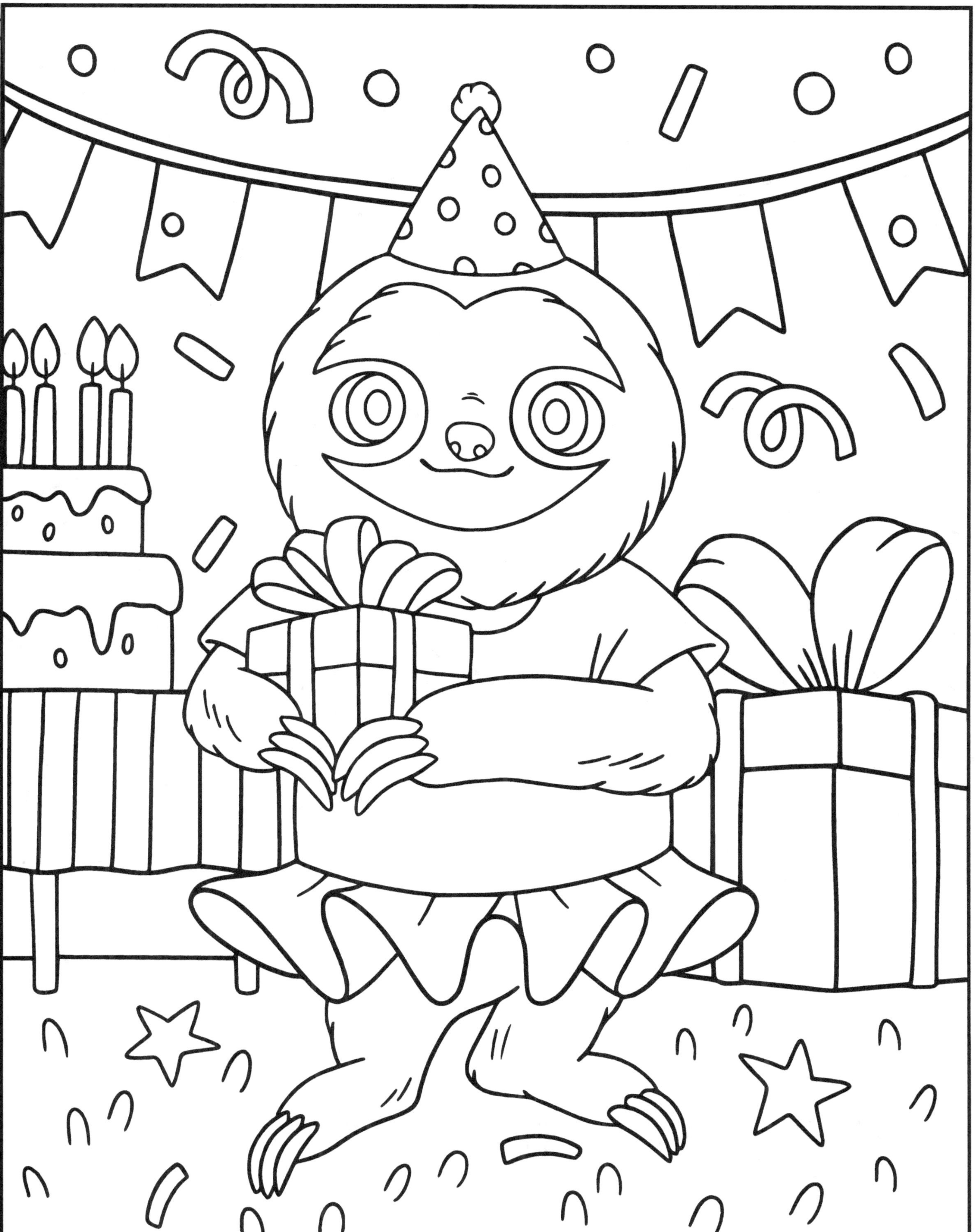

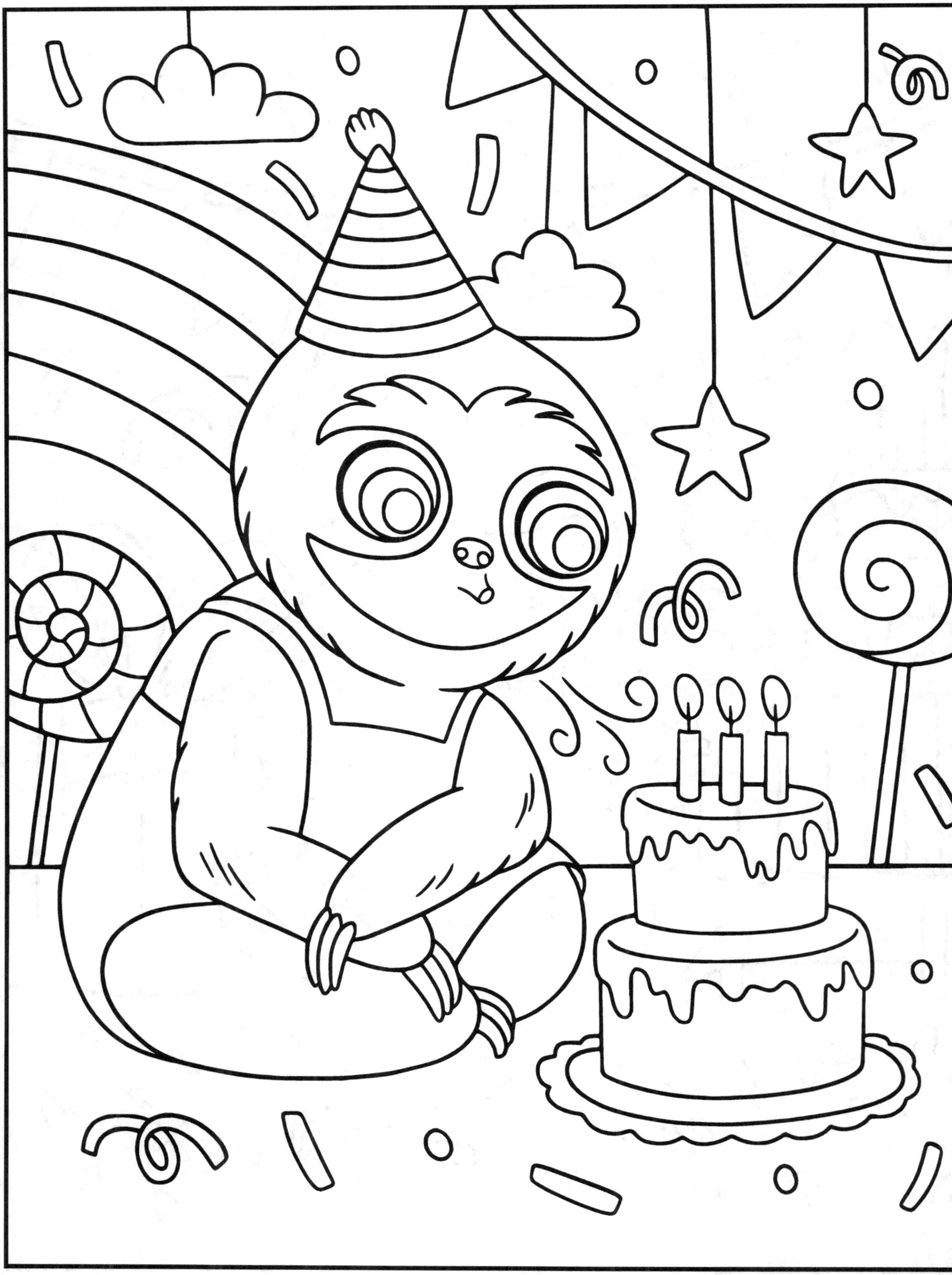

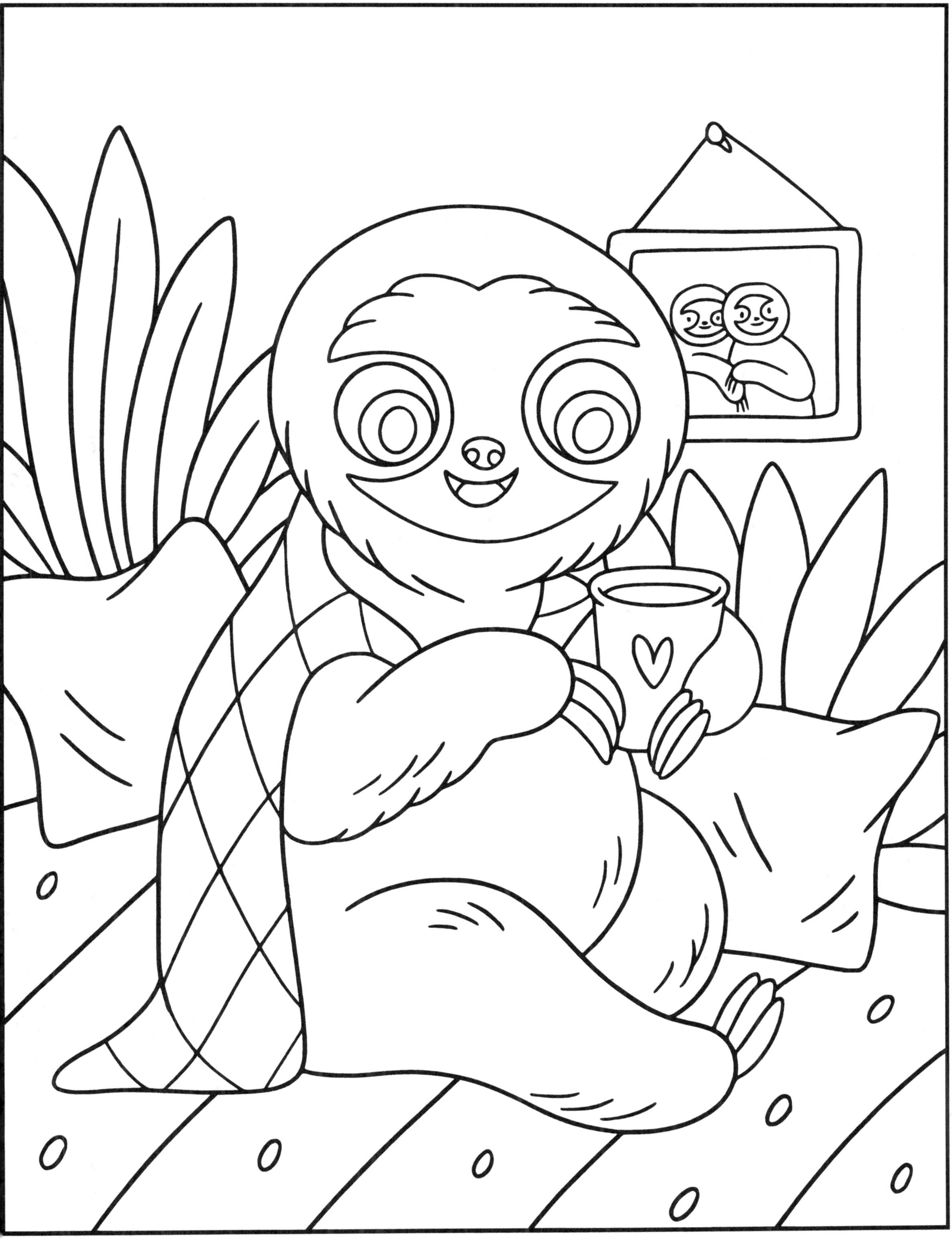

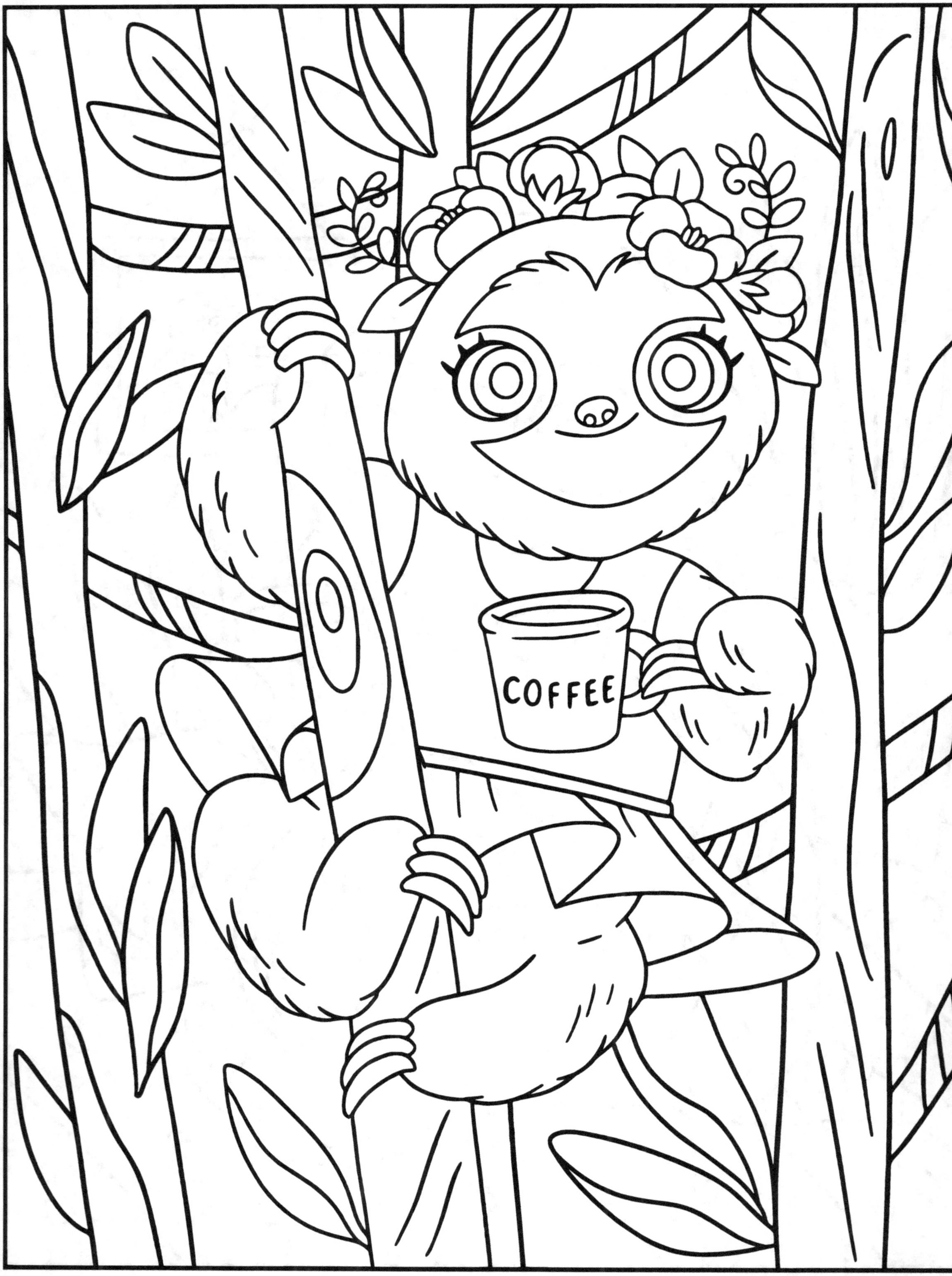
COFFEE

www.ingramcontent.com/pod-product-compliance
Lightning Source LLC
Chambersburg PA
CBHW080621220526
45466CB00010B/3415
* 9 7 9 8 5 9 0 0 4 5 0 3 7 *